From a Wooden Canoe

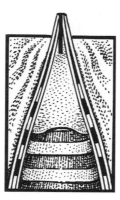

From a Wooden Canoe

Reflections on Canoeing, Camping, and Classic Equipment

JERRY DENNIS

Illustrations by Glenn Wolff

ST. MARTIN'S PRESS

NEW YORK

THOMAS DUNNE BOOKS.
An imprint of St. Martin's Press.

Portions of this book originally appeared, in somewhat different form, in the following publications: "Just Me and My Jacket" in *Traverse*; "Going Buggy" and "Dumb Moves" in *Silent Sports*; "A River by Any Name" in *Country Journal*; and "Paddling at Dawn" in *Sports Afield*. All other essays were first published in *Canoe and Kayak*.

Design by Ellen R. Sasahara

Library of Congress Cataloging-in-Publication Data

Dennis, Jerry.
    From a wooden canoe : reflections on canoeing, camping, and classic equipment / Jerry Dennis : illustrations by Glenn Wolff.—1st ed.
        p.   cm.
    "A Thomas Dunne book"—T.p. verso.
    ISBN 0-312-19979-1
    1. Canoes and canoeing 2. Camping. I. Title.
GV783.D46   1999
797.1'22—dc21   98-33238
                                                                      CIP

First Edition: March 1999

10 9 8 7 6 5 4 3 2 1

For
AARON AND NICK

Contents

Acknowledgments

My THANKS TO Graydon DeCamp at *Traverse* magazine, and Stephen Petit, formerly of *Canoe* magazine, for initiating the early columns that would eventually form the heart of this book.

Thanks also to Jan Nesset, managing editor of *Canoe and Kayak,* for rescuing "Traditions" when I had lost sight of it; Greg Marr at *Silent Sports* for encouraging me to develop related ideas for his readers; Tom Campbell at *Woods-N-Water News* for his enthusiasm and support; and Tim Bogardus, senior editor at *Sports Afield,* for appreciating the importance of canoeing on still lakes at dawn. Thanks to Craig Date, Mark Wilkes, and Mike McCumby for many great days on the water, to Scott Barkdoll for his insights on the art of building canoes and for providing the boat used on the dust jacket, and to Glenn Wolff for his friendship and extraordinary artistic talent. I'm deeply grateful as well to my editor, Pete Wolverton, and my agent, Michael Congdon, for recognizing a book when they saw one and helping hew it into shape.

Finally, special thanks to my wife, Gail, and my sons, Aaron and Nick, for tirelessly and cheerfully testing canoes, paddles, sleeping bags, union suits, freeze-dried and dehy-drated foods, portage yokes, tumplines, and roll after roll of duct tape. Without them I would never have found the soul in things, let alone the soul in myself.

Introduction

SECOND CHANCES DON'T come along often, so this book is a rare treat for me. Most of the essays gathered here first appeared in *Canoe and Kayak,* in a column I've contributed since 1990 called "Traditions." Assembling the columns in book form has allowed me to enlarge them, often to the length they cried out for in the first place. It has also given me the opportunity to tinker with their shape and timbre and give them a final polishing, a luxury that writers who work on deadline seldom enjoy.

The origin of "Traditions" was serendipitous in the extreme. It began with an invitation from Graydon DeCamp, an editor at *Traverse,* a lively and attractive magazine published in the small city near which I live, to write a brief essay in praise of my favorite item of outdoor clothing. I submitted a two-paragraph tribute to the red-and-black wool hunting jacket I'd been wearing for years. Shortly afterward, Stephen Petit, then a senior editor at *Canoe* (later to become *Canoe and Kayak*), asked if I would write a regular column in celebration of the things we cherish—the traditional equipment, tools, and clothing that are so much a part of our enjoyment of paddling and camping. It had been such fun writing about my old coat that I expanded those two paragraphs into my first "Traditions" column.

Although "Just Me and My Jacket" was collected in a previous book, *A Place on the Water,* where it found a home among reminiscences of growing up fishing and canoeing in northern Michigan, it is so integral to the present collection that I've decided to break with publishing protocol and include it here as well. It's near the front, tucked between "The Art of Portaging" and "Emporiums." I still have that old jacket, incidentally, but I regret to report that it no longer fits the way it once did. I keep it hanging in the basement stairway as a reminder of the durability of well-made things (as well as the mutability of the human body).

A note about the title. Friends who have explored the interior of my garage will have noticed that no wooden canoes are to be seen. A pair of Mad Rivers come nearest—a tandem Explorer and a solo Guide, both trimmed with gunwales, thwarts, and portage yokes of white ash and equipped with woven cane seats. Their hulls, however, are Royalex, not wood and canvas or cedar strips. I don't now own a wooden canoe, although that could change at any time. My only direct experience with such boats was when, at the age of sixteen, I helped rescue a tattered and weatherbeaten Old Town (which might have been a Chestnut or a Sears Roebuck) and then promptly destroyed it by stripping away the canvas and replacing it with fiberglass.

So, though I'm no expert on wooden boats, I've singled them out for the title of this book because they represent the spirit in which it was written. I hope readers devoted to building and maintaining classic canoes will forgive my presumptuousness.

My intention from the beginning was to write a tribute to wooden canoes and other things that don't go out of style, that resist obsolescence, that have been tested by time. In our fast-changing world it's still possible to find products that change slowly and that are built with integrity, passion, and attention to detail. Those values are contagious. They rub off on people. They offer relief from the shallow values of the automobile and fashion industries and the upgrade-or-die world of personal computers. In this time of great change, there's solace to be found in hardware that never needs upgrading.

Recently I asked some of my friends to list the possessions they've owned for twenty-five years and anticipate still owning twenty-five years from now. The answers were revealing. Everyone I spoke with mentioned wooden boats, musical instruments, antique furniture, old-time carpenter's tools, brass compasses, vintage cars, paintings, and sculpture. The common elements were quality and tradition. Almost without exception the objects that matter most to us are made of wood and metal. No plastic items were mentioned. No computers, televisions, or Jacuzzis made the cut. If I traveled in more prosperous circles, no doubt there would have been enthusiastic talk of Patek Philippe wristwatches, Ducati motorcycles, and Porsche 911s. Instead there were pocket watches and Harley-Davidsons and a 1910 lapstrake canoe.

With the exception of heirlooms that possess mainly sentimental value, we're usually willing to hang on to something for life only if it is useful or beautiful. When it possesses both those qualities it is probably because much time, thought, and effort went into designing and building it. If it's true that our possessions possess us, then it makes good sense to be possessed by things that work well and are pleasing to the senses.

We may clutter our homes with a thousand lesser possessions, but eventually we jettison everything that lacks lasting value. Those who die with the most toys do not necessarily win.

I HOPE THIS BOOK serves as a kind of walking tour through some of the good things and simple pleasures of the outdoor life. Call me old-fashioned, but I'd like the pace to slow a bit. I'd like to see people take time to appreciate what matters. Maybe this is pigheadedness on my part, but I'm convinced that the world looks better from a wooden canoe.

From a Wooden Canoe

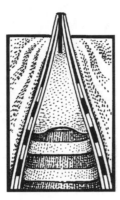

Wooden Canoes

CANOES ARE PERFECT FOR SNEAKING UP ON THE world. If you spend a lot of time on the water and are vigilant and lucky, you're certain to be rewarded with wonderful perceptions—the glint of starlight on a lake, the splashing liquid motion of an otter, the way the setting sun paints the water with swirls of orange and gold. The pace of a canoe makes us see with wider eyes and listen with better ears. Every bend in a river and every wooded point on a lake becomes an opportunity to encounter the unexpected.

Any canoe will do for such encounters, but the best for the job are wooden ones. This is personal opinion, of course, and not easily defensible. If I were a true traditionalist I would paddle a canoe of birchbark or a hollowed log. And I recognize that the modern revolution in synthetic materials has created canoes of unexcelled durability and superb performance. What I'm talking about is something else altogether. Call it soul.

It's probably a romantic conceit to believe that wood has soul while fiberglass, aluminum, and plastic do not. But there is a crucial difference between wood and synthetic materials:

Wood was once alive. It was a supple, growing thing, shaped by wind and rain into a one-of-a-kind material with heart. You can see the uniqueness in its grain, feel the heart of it in the grip and heft of a gunwale or paddle shaft. There are qualities involved that can never be reproduced synthetically.

It takes time to appreciate such qualities. Skin-deep beauty is easy to find, but to recognize it at its deepest and most enduring levels you have to invest a great deal of time in close contact with it. Spend hours playing a fine old Gibson mandolin and you gradually come to recognize its superiority to other mandolins—how subtle and bright its tones are, how responsive it is to individual styles of play. A similar responsiveness exists in any good tool, canoes included. At first, except for its appearance, a wood-and-canvas or wood-strip canoe might not seem special. It might seem clumsy compared to a Kevlar racer or fragile compared to a Royalex tripper. But paddle it all day, and you witness a transformation. The virtues of those other boats are in mechanical characteristics that make them efficient, fast, and durable. The wooden boat's virtues are less utilitarian and less tangible. Instead of characteristics, it has character. Instead of following the shortest distance between two points, it meanders. You can hear it hum and whisper as it slices the water. It seems to come alive beneath you.

The wonder is not that canoes are light, responsive craft that can be paddled over a river or lake with relative ease, but that they can be paddled at all. Water is not an ideal medium of transportation. Its molecular structure is such that a foreign object tends to cling to it, to be stopped by it, to be swallowed by it. Flotation is a relatively simple process, achieved by predictable steps. Elegant passage requires more effort. It requires a design shaped by water and refined by the ages. That refinement—the graceful evocation of form by function—explains why canoes are beautiful.

The essayist E. B. White had a few things to say on the subject of functional beauty. "I do not recall," he wrote, "ever seeing a properly designed boat that was not also a beautiful boat. Purity of line, loveliness, symmetry—these arrive mysteriously whenever someone who knows and cares creates something that is perfectly fitted to do its work." The late paddling sage Bill Mason felt similar reverence for properly designed boats. He went so far as to call the canoe "the simplest, most functional, yet aesthetically pleasing object ever created."

Mason did not specify which kind of canoe he had in mind, but it's a good bet he meant a wooden one, a direct descendent of those built by the woodland Indians. The bark canoes of the first Americans were built on frameworks of white cedar, black spruce, maple, or ash that were astonishingly similar to the frames of modern canoes. Indian boatbuilders, who understood how hull shape and size affect speed and performance, built specialized craft for such purposes as maneuvering in whitewater rivers, crossing open lakes where high wind and waves were a hazard, transporting large amounts of cargo, traveling at high speed, and hunting and fishing. Many of their designs, perfected through a hundred generations of trial and error, are still used in modern canoes. Each is part of a continuum; paddling one is a way to reach across the centuries.

If your purpose in going out on the water is to get as far as possible from the linear, nine-to-five place where you earn a living, there is no better boat for you than one built without concern for clocks. So much time goes into the construction of a wooden boat that it is the kind of project often saved until retirement or for long winters or other fallow periods. It is not a job you want to tally in hours and dollars. The people who build such boats commercially are far more concerned with tradition and craftsmanship than with profit.

In our culture, where anything new is automatically assumed to be better, it is considered a kind of blasphemy to argue for traditional ways of doing things. But, as canoe builders have known for hundreds of years, sometimes the old ways are the best ways. Sometimes we need to be gloriously impractical. Sometimes we need to find the soul in things before we can find the soul in ourselves.

The Scent of Canvas

A TENT IS MORE THAN JUST SHELTER FROM RAIN AND wind and insects, it's a temporary home. When we make camp we erect a roof of nylon or canvas, cut and stack firewood, procure drinking water, and cook a meal—usually in that order. We often stop short of hanging pictures on the walls and nailing a mailbox to a tree out front, but clearly we're trying to make a home for ourselves, a place where we are safe, at ease, comfortable.

Tent manufacturers know this and take pains to make their products as comfortable and attractive as possible. The revolution in camping equipment during the past twenty years has made it possible for almost anyone to afford a tent that is waterproof, sturdy, quick to set up, and light enough to be carried easily. When the weather turns bad and every pound counts, you can thank the stars—or the wizards at Sierra Designs—for the roof over your head.

Yet I'm struck by how little sanctuary is required to satisfy the homing instinct. A carefully excavated snow shelter or a lean-to of saplings and tarpaulin can seem as luxurious as an Adirondack lodge, one with a guesthouse, a front porch, and a fireplace big enough to roast a hog. The satisfaction of a good camp rises in proportion to the amount of time and effort you put into it, but you don't always need a state-of-the-art mountaineering tent to feel well sheltered.

When I was a kid we used only two types of tents, A-frame pup tents for sleeping one or two, and wall tents for groups. Both were made of canvas. Canvas is cloth with backbone; it's the fabric equivalent of oak. It holds firm beneath heavy snow and stands before wind that would shred lesser materials. When you bed down under canvas, you become steeped in its smell, the musty fragrance of army-surplus shops and old gear stored in utility closets. Even its flaws are charming: Run a finger down the wall and condensation wicks through like nectar.

Canvas is woven coarsely of such fibers as cotton, flax, and hemp and in its various forms is strong enough to serve for sails, tennis shoes, duffel bags, tarpaulins, and tents. Drill is an inexpensive canvas that weighs six to seven ounces per square yard, more if the fabric has been treated with weatherproofing. Poplin is sturdy and windproof, with a weight of about six ounces per square yard. Duck is the canvas made famous by such military applications as duffels, ammo bags, and wall tents; its fill and warp are doubled and twisted before weaving, making it among the most durable of all fabrics but heavy— about ten ounces per square yard. Balloon silk is not silk, and it doesn't balloon (except in heavy winds), but is a canvas woven from Egyptian cotton. This lightweight material (four or five ounces per yard) is strong for its weight and was the fabric of choice for most campers at the turn of the twentieth century. It was exceeded in quality and expense only by silk, which is extremely lightweight—a London advertisement for a one-person silk tent in the 1890s claimed that it weighed under twelve ounces—and can be woven so tightly that it needs no further treatment to remain waterproof.

One of the things I like about canvas in general is that a square of it is so useful. Fitted with grommets and tie loops it can be draped over a rope stretched between two trees, staked to the ground at four corners, and it becomes a serviceable and nearly indestructible emergency shelter. Rig it as a lean-to or wrap it around a turned-over canoe, and it becomes a good shelter on summer nights. Extend it in an awning between trees, and you have a dry place to cook when it's raining. Lash it over your gear in a boat, and it makes an effective splash guard. Spread it on snow, and you have a rug on which you can roll up your sleeping bag, change your clothes, and wrestle with your dog. A ten-by-ten-foot canvas tarpaulin is too heavy to fold into a backpack, and it can't serve any purpose that a square of polyethylene can't serve, but it's a chunk of tradition in camp. And it's got that smell.

When you buy canvas tents and tarps today, they come already waterproofed. If your tent starts to leak, you can treat the seams with two coats of Thompson's Water Seal and you won't have to worry for years (this excellent tip comes from Cliff Jacobson's *The Basic Essentials of Trailside Shelters*). It's easy to take waterproofing for granted. We forget that a generation or two ago it was no easy matter to prepare a tent for harsh weather. In 1897, Perry Frazier's *Canoe Cruising and Camping* offered the best advice of the day on ways to make canvas shed water. The initial suggestions in the list below are the simplest but also the least effective; the latter ones, though more effective, become correspondingly more complicated, until the final recipe resembles a formula in an alchemist's notebook:

1. A coat of boiled linseed oil will render [canvas] nearly waterproof; two will make it waterproof, but somewhat heavier.

2. Dissolve paraffin in naphtha or benzine, and soak the goods thoroughly in the solution.

3. Dissolve a half pound of sugar of lead and a half pound of powdered alum in a bucket of rainwater, and pour off into another vessel; steep the canvas in it, but let it soak thoroughly. Hang canvas up and let it dry, but do not wring it. Add to the quantity in same proportion, if insufficient.

4. Take 11 pounds of alum and 11 pounds of sugar of lead; dissolve in 10 ⅗ quarts of boiling water. Pour both solutions, while hot, into a wooden dish, whereby a white precipitate of lead takes place. Let it cool; then draw the fluid off; dilute it as needed with 53 quarts of water. Then dissolve in water 17½ ounces of isinglass, or 5 ½ pounds of white glue. Pour the first solution into the latter. Let the canvas soak in this solution over night. Hang up to dry without wringing.

Every October a dozen old friends and I make a hunting camp in Michigan's Upper Peninsula. Though we sleep in separate quarters, the heart of our camp is a wall tent so large we can gather inside to eat our meals and play cards. The tent is too heavy and bulky to carry on our backs or in a canoe, but that is not an issue at this camp. We transport it in a truck and have plenty of willing arms to wrestle it to the ground and set it up. After the poles have been fitted and raised and the stakes driven into the ground and the guy ropes adjusted, we always make one or two additional circuits to tighten every line and give the canvas the snappy tautness necessary to repel water. It takes some time, but once it's up it's there to stay. We use it for only a week, but it could easily last the winter. With chairs and tables and a couple of suspended lanterns, it becomes a kind of community house. When it rains or when early snow sweeps down from Lake Superior, we hang our wet clothes inside and stand around drinking coffee and planning future hunts.

Such tents have limitations, of course. For expeditions on foot or in paddle craft, canvas tents are best left folded on a shelf in the garage. I'd hate to give up my nylon dome tent with its waterproof fly, its shock-corded poles, its windproof zippers, and its sealed seams. I don't miss the tent of my youth—a floorless canvas wedge supported by an armload of ropes, stakes, and wooden poles—and the water and mosquitoes that were always finding their way inside. But sometimes the new-car aroma of nylon tents makes me nostalgic for the earthy, all's-well-with-the-world scent of canvas.

Memory can't always be trusted in these matters, but it seems to me that I have never slept as well as I did in the canvas wall tent my friends and I set up in the field behind Ken Norris's house when we were twelve years old. We slept in the tent two or three nights a week that summer, staying up late telling stories and inventing dreams for the future, then falling one after another into sleep so profound it was like a distillation of all the purity and innocence of childhood itself. I remember waking in the morning, nested deep in my sleeping bag, and breathing the odors of canvas and freshly cut hay. The sun was high enough to warm the walls and make the inside of the tent glow with emerald light. Birds sang in the trees outside, as if announcing the arrival of something too marvelous to miss, and I jumped up and threw open the canvas flaps and stood amazed and dazzled by this latest bright wonder: a new day.

Matchless Matches

I WAS NOT THE MOST ARDENT OF BOY SCOUTS, BEING from an early age suspicious of khaki uniforms and blank-faced youths standing in ranks reciting slogans. Also, I had an uninspiring scoutmaster. He was tired all the time, seemed uninterested in kids, and was a born-again Christian. We spent most of each week's meeting sitting in a circle in his living room memorizing the books of the Old and New Testaments. Never mind the contents, just learn the names, recite them from memory in the correct order, and you got a merit badge to sew on your shirt. It was one of only two merit badges I earned during my tenure as a Scout. (The other, perhaps as a consequence of all the talk about hell, was in fire-starting.) I learned two things from weary Mr. Skinner: Obadiah follows Amos, and a good Scout never goes into the woods without a supply of matches.

Those Monday nights while Mr. Skinner droned on about our souls and Mrs. Skinner shuffled around the kitchen in a worn housedress, I learned to think of matches as a subject worthy of reverence. I adored them. For years I kept them in my pockets, backpack, tackle box, and school locker. I stashed them against unforseen emergencies in my dresser drawer and in the handle grips of my bicycle. While other boys my age favored them for lighting up the occasional bent cigarette—Mike Sheffer kept a cluster in the pocket of his jeans for that purpose, until one day at school he was running on the playground and friction set them off; that boy could *dance*—I wanted them for the ready utility of their flame, for their perfect merging of form and function.

Wooden matches—especially the large, strike-anywhere kitchen variety best represented by Ohio Blue Tips, those Oldsmobiles of matches—are such fine products that improvement is unimaginable. They're potent suckers, splendid embodiments of potential energy, upstanding, raring to go, perky, and self-important, with their white-capped blue heads just daring you to drag them snappily across a rough surface. Scratch 'em and they flare, a two-stage hissing, smoking explosion that calms in a second to steady flame. They smell of brimstone and the illicit sensual pleasures of childhood.

Today's matches are descended from an unreliable strike-anywhere invented in 1827 by an English pharmacist. It was much improved in 1830 by a Frenchman named Charles Suria, who used white phosphorus in the tip to create a stronger, more dependable match known as a lucifer, or "light bearer," for the eponymous fallen archangel. Suria's lucifer was in widespread use until about the end of the nineteenth century, but it had the unpleasant habit of occasionally killing people with its poisonous fumes. The public demanded improvements. Strike-anywhere and book matches as we know them came along soon afterward, and the world became a brighter and safer place.

But although they have been greatly improved, they're not perfect. Moisture has been the bane of matches since their invention. My old camp-lore books suggest waterproofing wooden matches by dipping them in a solution of shellac and alcohol, or by setting them head-down in an empty shotgun shell or other canister and covering them with liquefied candle wax. I've tried the candle-wax tactic, and it works fine. A kitchen match treated with wax repels water admirably, even after being soaked for hours in a wet pocket. A single scratch, and it ignites with gusto. The wax makes the flame sputter for a moment, like a four-cylinder engine with bad spark plugs, but it always erupts finally in confident flame.

Many commercially produced waterproof matches are available, and most are excellent. I've used a couple of brands under tough conditions—hunkered beneath dripping hemlocks, for instance, after canoeing all day in the rain—and with the exception of one box of Chinese cheapos that kept breaking off at the heads, they've all performed masterfully. But I can't say they're any better than the homemade versions. And they're a lot more expensive, which bothers me.

Maybe I've been spoiled by the bounty of all those free packs handed out at restaurants and motels, but it seems to me that matches are one product we should be able to waste with impunity. Ohio Blue Tips sell in boxes of 250 for about a buck. That's 2.5 matches to the penny. At that price you can burn them for the fun of it or chew them the way James Dean did, rolling them from one corner of his mouth to the other, spitting out the soggy splinters when they came apart.

At night, sitting around a campfire, I like to ignite matches just to watch the way people react. Swipe one across a stone and everyone stares. Our eyes go automatically to the flame and stay there as long as it burns. We can't help ourselves. We're fascinated. If we were moths we would gladly scorch our wings for a closer orbit.

The Art of Portaging

YOU CAN BE SURE THE WORLD IS GETTING TOO CIVILIZED
when all the portage trails are marked with signs. I know, I
know: The herds must be kept on the path so they don't
erode the banks and trample endangered wildflowers. And
yes, signs are convenient, especially at dusk, when getting lost
means spending an uncomfortable night in the woods.

But I miss the days when you *could* get lost, when the
faint trail around a rapids branched off into three or four traces
that led to hidden huckleberry thickets where you could happily spend an afternoon staining your smile blue. I miss finding
my own way across a carry and, better yet, lucking on to
ancient rutted trails that might have been blazed by Ojibwa
hunters and deepened by voyageurs in the days of flintlocks
and birchbarks. I don't want a sign to point it out. I want to
discover it myself.

To the voyageurs who explored the old Northwest and
opened up much of the continent to white settlers, portaging
was a necessary inconvenience. They followed old trails
marked with "lob-trees"—tall pines stripped of their top
branches so they stood like exclamation marks against the

sky—completing the trek as quickly and efficiently as possible. According to Grace Lee Nute in her 1931 study, *The Voyageur,* those tough French Canadians were usually under five feet six inches, to take up as little space in a canoe as possible, yet could heft two or three and sometimes as many as five ninety-pound cargo bags on their backs, cinch them with a tumpline, and jog across portages. Typically they would trot about a third of a mile, put down their load, and go back for another. Those legs of the trip, or *posés,* were used to measure the length of a portage. One forty-five-mile portage in Wisconsin consisted of one hundred twenty-two *posés.* Other difficult trails, like the nine-mile Grand Portage around the falls of the Pigeon River, and the twelve-mile Methye Portage on the Saskatchewan River, took on legendary status and became gauges of endurance. If you could portage a freight canoe and all its cargo across the Methye in a single day you were indeed a voyageur and not some flabby flatland porkeater.

Bruised feet, twisted ankles, and severe hernias were common among the voyageurs, but only the worst injuries kept them from their work. They did much of their traveling in birchbarks twenty-five feet long or longer, too large and too heavy to be carried easily, so whenever a portage could be avoided, it was. Rapids were often run, even when forbidden by fur-company regulations. Sometimes a rapids or obstruction could be bypassed by unloading the passengers and some of the freight and lining the boat down the river with a rope, or *cordelle.* To *cordelle* around a difficult stretch of water saved time and effort but frequently resulted in damaged canoes and lost cargo.

Everyone I know has a love-hate affair with portages. Most of us can't even make up our minds whether to pronounce the word as the French "por-TAJ" and risk sounding pretentious, or blurt out the Anglicized "POR-tidge" and risk sounding provincial. However you pronounce it, it's plain hard work. Humping a seventy-five-pound canoe and a sixty-pound pack over a winding, uneven, hilly, rock-strewn, log-obstructed, mud-sucking, mosquito-laced, back-woods trail is nobody's idea of fun. Bill Mason said it's like hitting yourself on the head with a hammer (because it feels so good when you stop). My old paddling partner Craig Date keeps his mind off the pain of tough portages by chanting a chorus of "son of a bitches" every step of the way.

Yet there is something about it we love. Portaging separates us from casual day-trippers and picnickers. Every step takes us farther from highways and houses and deeper into wildness, on trails that were sometimes already ancient when they were used by voyageurs, missionaries, and explorers early in the eighteenth century. The indefatigable Sigurd Olson, a veteran of thousands of carries in the Quetico-Superior country of Minnesota and Ontario, considered portaging an opportunity "to hear sounds that are lost on the water, see things that until then have been hidden." Even those of us who don't grow lyrical in praise of portages recognize their virtues. They exercise not just muscles but commitment, are proof of the heart we carry with us into the wild. Portaging in these days of Kevlar canoes, freeze-dried dinners, and compact camping equipment is not the grueling ordeal it was in the eighteenth century, but at the end of a mile-long carry your aching muscles can make you feel you've earned a place in one of those twenty-five-foot voyageurs' canoes.

ONE GOOD WAY to make portaging less of an ordeal is to use good tools for the job. For years I relied on army-surplus duffel bags to carry my gear in canoes and across portages, and was frequently mystified by the phenomenon of infinitely expanding camping equipment. At the start of every expedition my sleeping bag, tent, spare clothes, cook kit, food, and all miscellaneous necessities fit into a pair of World War II army-surplus duffel bags. The look of all that gear packed so tidily made me feel virtuous, lean, and mobile.

Only thing was, by the time I reached the first portage I had already gotten hungry, pulled a few things out of the bags, and suddenly, instead of two duffels stuffed tight as bratwursts, I had two duffels tight as bratwursts plus a plastic bag filled with snack foods, a rigged fly rod, a rain jacket, a camera, an ax, and a bottle of insect repellent, all spread across the bottom of my canoe. And every item needed to be gathered and carried across the portage.

In their favor, duffel bags are durable and stack nicely between the thwarts. Beyond that, I can think of no reason to recommend them. You can't carry one for long before you're forced to sling it to the other shoulder, and there seems no way at all to carry one on your back to free both hands for other gear. Don't even think about hauling a duffel and a canoe simultaneously.

One day I had a revelation: Duluth packs work. For years I had thought they were nothing but duffels with sensible straps. I'm reminded of my surprise at discovering as a college sophomore that it's fun to read Shakespeare. The realization took time to sink in, but eventually it occurred to me that classics become classics because they deserve it.

This particular classic has been manufactured since 1911 by the Duluth Tent and Awning Company in Duluth, Minnesota. From the beginning it's been made of fifteen-ounce canvas, in a variety of sizes (I especially like the twenty-eight-by-twenty-seven-inch model #3, which is big enough for a sleeping bag, tent, tarp, and cook kit), and comes equipped with wide leather shoulder straps, leather flap closures, and a tumpline, all anchored to the canvas with hand-hammered copper rivets. It's designed to ride comfortably and low on your back, allowing enough room to fit a canoe's portage yoke over your shoulders. It's also compact, with a low center of balance that keeps it upright in a canoe, with only a few inches showing above the gunwales and only the bottom subject to the ravages of bilge water. Two or three of them nestle together nicely for long expeditions and adjust easily to the contours of a canoe; one strapped to a thwart is perfect for a weekend trip in a solo boat. Some models have one or two individual pockets, but it's easier to waterproof a single compartment (line it with a heavy-gauge plastic garbage bag). The top opens wide to give quick access to the contents, making it possible to get at the topographical map on the bottom without pulling everything else out first. Thus the problem of infinitely expanding equipment is solved.

Duluth packs are often compared—sometimes favorably, sometimes not—to that other venerable packing system, the Maine pack basket. This upright basket, woven from strips of black ash, was made for centuries by Native Americans, but is now sometimes available in factory-made versions. Traditionalists demand that their packs be constructed of strips of black ash that have been split along the tree's growth rings. Commercial versions made of white ash and palm rattan are inferior and tend to break apart under hard use. Like the Duluth pack, the ash pack basket rides upright in a canoe, has shoulder harnesses, and is durable, but it has the added advantage of protecting breakable items. A few paddlers, in an East-meets-Midwest effort to promote unity, have combined the two systems by inserting the Maine basket inside the Duluth pack.

The wanigan is another traditional packing and portaging

system that deserves mention. This hard, waterproof box, sometimes called a tote box or grub box, is designed to rest on the bottom of a canoe. If equipped with shoulder straps and tumpline it can be portaged, though the sharp corners and hard exterior sometimes result in "wanigan bite" when the bottom edge digs into the small of your back. It is usually the least popular item on every portage. Made of wood or plastic, and sometimes built with rounded bottoms to follow hull contours, it is most useful for transporting food, kitchen gear, cameras, fishing tackle, and other fragile items. In its favor it serves multiple purposes around camp, most notably as a cutting board, serving table, and bench.

The new breed of dry bags made of PVC-coated vinyl (polyvinyl chloride) are basically improved duffel bags, fully waterproof, tough, and decked out with functional though not very comfortable shoulder straps and hip belts. Those I've tried seem to satisfy most of the functions of a Duluth pack, and require no additional protection against leakage. They might prove to be the classics of the next century.

But I have a soft spot for my Duluth pack. It's grown better with the years, fading to a gentle forest olive, the leather richer and more supple than ever, the fabric worn soft as old blue jeans. I like the look, feel, and smell of it. It's dependable. It promises to last a lifetime. It feels good on my back.

Portaging awakens us to the hard old way of doing things. Every jolting step, every arrow of pain, every aching muscle reminds us that we're not far removed from life as it was lived centuries ago. Carrying our equipment from one waterway to another makes us stronger and more independent. Every portage takes us another step away from the frenetic and mind-numbing world of commuter airlines and cellular phones. We don't want it to be easy. A PORTAGE HERE sign is an announcement that we've gotten soft, that there are too many of us, that the great American wilderness has been packaged up and parceled off forever. Who wants to be reminded of that?

Just Me and My Jacket

M<small>Y WIFE CAN'T UNDERSTAND WHY I CHOOSE TO</small> remain ignorant of outdoor fashions. Contrary to what she thinks, I do not hate clean clothes or hope secretly for opportunities to roll around in mud. I admit I prefer well-worn clothing, but I don't necessarily want it unwashed. It's true that as a child I slept with my dog, but not until he had dried off from the day's explorations and never if he had rooted around that day in the fish that sometimes washed up dead on the beach near our house. I may be a bit of a slob, but I have standards.

The truth is, when it comes to clothing, I just can't keep up with technology. While many of my friends have been converted to Gore-Tex and Thermax and those other super-synthetics that were discovered accidentally in corporate laboratories and tested in outer space, my favorite article of clothing remains a red-and-black wool hunting jacket. It's a garment essentially unchanged since the days of ax-slinging lumberjacks. My grandfather wore one just like it, along with red wool pants that fastened snugly around his ankles. Seeing me in my jacket, Gail once suggested that in a previous life I inhabited an unchinked log cabin near James Bay and passed my days on snowshoes, tending a trapline and making smoked jerky out of hunks of moose meat. It's an attractive idea.

Any jacket as dependable, warm, and comforting as mine is worth defending to the death. Unlike the modern synthetic models I've handled, mine is pleasantly heavy. You know you're wearing it. It's as satisfying to heft around on your shoulders as a well-loaded backpack. It's durable in the manner of good leather boots, and it's equipped with so many pockets I'm still discovering new ones. Pockets are important to me. I like to put my hands inside and be surprised at what I find: a flattened pack of Doublemint, a book of impotent matches, pinecones, fossils, a berserk compass, one jersey glove, a magnifying glass, a 20-gauge shotgun shell, a grouse feather, a packet of crumpled and arcane notes to myself. Whenever any small but important object comes up missing around home, my kids automatically look in Dad's jacket pockets. Even if it's not there they come away contented, certain to have discovered something of equal or greater value.

These days, when so many people outdoors appear to have stepped from the pages of an L. L. Bean catalog and invariably examine the labels on your clothing before they meet your eyes, it's satisfying to believe fashion is irrelevant. I want functional clothing that leaps beyond trends to comfort and durability. My jacket is appropriate whether I'm canoeing on brisk September mornings or fishing for December steelhead; it works equally well for grouse hunting, cross-country skiing, hiking, or cutting firewood. When camping I roll it inside a cotton sweatshirt and it becomes a pillow. In a pinch I could use it to smother a brushfire or signal a rescue plane. I can wad it, beat it, wipe my hands on it, drag it through brambles, toss it in a corner, stand on it barefoot while drying my socks over a fire, even spill Craig Date's industrial-formula

Texas chili on it without fear of spontaneous combustion. If I were desperate enough, I suspect I could boil it down into a nutritious broth. It never berates me for the abuse it suffers, and it stays warm even when wet. And when wet it smells— faintly, just enough to recall old friends—like a wet golden retriever.

I realize my jacket needs washing, and has for several years, but the label under the collar says it must be dry-cleaned, and I don't trust the chemical processes used in dry-cleaning. Besides, you can't actually notice it needs washing unless you get very close. The red-and-black color scheme is designed to mask stains, and when dirty the wool improves in wearability and maybe even increases in insulation value.

My jacket and I will probably never be asked to model for the cover of GQ, but we can live with that. I figure it's the fashion world's loss.

Emporiums

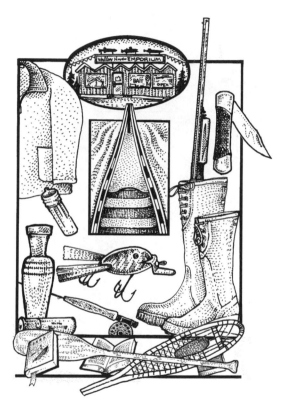

CANOES, PADDLES, TENTS, AND FLY RODS ARE NOT
mere implements of sport. They're badges of our passions,
part of the way we think about ourselves. So it's not surprising
that we like to hang out in places where we can buy such
things. Shops that specialize in good stuff are such a delight
to visit that they can become community centers for like-
minded people.

I was born near the end of the era of classic outdoor stores,
those repositories of everything an outdoors person could
want. The ones I remember most fondly were old, with high,
hammered-tin ceilings and dusty glass windows and wooden
counters worn smooth from generations of forearms. Tools
and hardware were in the front, fishing and hunting gear in
the back, and in between were shadowy nooks cluttered with
wheelbarrows, bicycles, chainsaws, and stepladders. Each
store had a canoe or two suspended on wires from the ceiling,
a selection of wooden paddles stacked in a barrel in a corner,
and racks of shelves filled with tents, leather boots, hunting
jackets, shotgun and rifle shells, fishing lures, reels, duck de-
coys, kerosene lanterns, hatchets, snowshoes, and spare parts

for a dozen makes of obsolete outboard motors. No matter what you were looking for—say a bail spring for a South Bend spinning reel or a recoil pad for a Remington auto-loader—the owner of the shop would say, "I've got one here somewhere" and start pawing through boxes on a shelf. More often than not he found it.

Some stores more closely resembled museums than retail outlets. In a free-standing case of mahogany and glass were dozens of compartments filled with trout flies tied by the proprietor's uncle; another held a framed display of hunting knives. On a back wall hung army-surplus haversacks and gas masks and in a corner leaned bundles of wooden tent poles. Against another wall was an ancient, hunched refrigerator loaded with cottage-cheese containers filled with night-crawlers. Beside it were two or three galvanized tubs of water filled with tirelessly circling minnows.

In winter a cast-iron woodstove gave off waves of heat and was tended by old men sitting around it in kitchen chairs talking about how much better everything used to be. A customer with questions could always count on those sage experts for detailed and contradictory advice about plumbing, automobile repair, and places to go fishing and hunting. On a table near the stove an aluminum percolator as big as a trash can sighed and muttered and exhaled the scent of well-cooked coffee. The store was underlit and overheated, crowded with goods from floor to ceiling, and smelled of leather and old canvas, of mothballs and dust, of damp wool and wet dogs. It smelled like my grandfather's closet.

OUR TOWN HAD several such stores. One that nearly fit the description, though without the woodstove or the free coffee and offering beer, soft drinks, and men's magazines instead of plumbing supplies, was presided over by a tall, glowering man who hated kids. Drawn to the place but afraid of the man, I would usually go there only in the company of my father. But the store was located only a few blocks from the lower Boardman River and was the nearest source of hooks and split shot when I was dropped off to fish the river on days when my parents came to town to shop. If I ran short of tackle, I walked to the store and made a modest purchase. I always braved the suspicious gaze of the tall man at the counter to look over the racks of Creek Chubs, Rapalas, Mepps spinners, and other lures I could not afford to buy.

The shop was an official weighing station for a fishing contest sponsored for years by our chamber of commerce. If you caught a fish that exceeded dimensions established for each species—five pounds for smallmouth bass, six pounds for walleye, ten pounds for northern pike and steelhead trout—you took it to be weighed on the massive white butcher's scale at the checkout counter, received official authorization from the proprietor, and were later mailed an attractive ceramic plaque printed with your name and a description of the fish. I had already received plaques for walleye and bass and had hung them on the wall of our family room, where visitors could not miss them. I wanted more.

One morning I caught a large steelhead in the Boardman. It struggled fiercely, lunging deep in the current below the Front Street Bridge. I fought it until it tired, then led it upstream, netted it, and laid it on the ground to admire. It was the largest steelhead I had ever caught. There was no doubt about what I had to do. I clobbered the fish on the head with a stick, grabbed it through the gills, and set off on foot for the store.

When I pushed through the door, struggling with my rod in one hand and the big trout in the other, the owner looked up from the counter. He was not thrilled to see me.

"That fish dead?"

"Yep, I whacked him good."

I brought the trout to the counter and tried to heft it onto the scale, but my arm was cramped from carrying the fish, and I couldn't lift it high enough. The guy made unpleasant noises and leaned across the counter to help. He grasped the fish by the head and tail. It trembled in a mild spasm.

"You sure this is dead?"

"I hit him on the head with a stick."

"Well, I hope you hit him hard."

He lowered the trout into the basket of the scale and released his hold. The pointer swung past ten pounds and hovered there. It was a winner. The guy filled out an authorization slip and gave it to me. He scowled. I grinned. The trout thumped its tail, arched, and slid off the scale. It rode across the counter on a trail of slime and knocked a display of cigarettes to the floor.

The man bellowed. He grabbed the fish with both hands and threw it at me, like a basketball player making a two-handed pass. I did what anyone would do, I ducked, and the steelhead struck a floor rack of potato chips and sent every bag flying down the aisle.

I ran. I scooped the trout into my arms, cradled it with my rod and the document authorizing my angling prowess, and ran out the door. The guy shouted that I should never come back. He shouted other things, too, but that was what stuck in my mind. I was disappointed because I liked his store. But I got over it. The chamber of commerce mailed the plaque a week or two later. It still hangs in my parents' house.

. . .

THESE DAYS MOST of the old outdoor emporiums have gone the way of corner groceries and neighborhood barbershops. They've been replaced, if that's the word, by Dunhams, Gander Mountain, REI, and other anchors of our strip-mall culture. You have to look hard and long to find a shop where people hang out to talk and kill time. We're lucky where I live to have the Troutsman, a fly shop owned by my friend Kelly Galloup, where the coffee is always on and you're always welcome to sit at the big table in back and watch the resident wits tie flies and tell lies about the giant fish they've caught. Times have changed, though. Nobody comes in looking for minnows or sheer pins for 1938 Johnson outboards or advice about running copper lines in their bathrooms. Most of the young men and women who come in to shop for Patagonia fleece jackets and Sage graphite rods have never heard of the wall plaques the chamber of commerce once gave out for trophy fish.

It's just as well. Many of us release the big ones these days, and when we swing by Kelly's shop for a cup of coffee and start bragging about ten-pound steelhead, we'd better have photos to back it up. A dead fish in the trunk impresses nobody, and a plaque with our name on it is not considered admissible evidence.

All Hail the Union Suit

ACCORDING TO LEGEND, OLD-TIME PROSPECTORS, cowboys, and lumberjacks wore the same pair of long underwear from autumn until spring because of an aversion to bathwater. I know better. After wearing a red union suit during a wet and unseasonably cold October in the Upper Peninsula, I'm convinced there's another reason: because they're warm, comfortable, and comforting, like the one-piece bunny pajamas or Dr. Denton's you wore when you were three.

I've been a fan of red union suits since a night many years ago in Yellowstone Park when my wife and I heard a sudden racket of shouting and banging pots and pans from the campsite next to ours. We turned a spotlight in that direction and watched a large black bear insert its claws into the door of our neighbor's pickup camper, rip it off its hinges, and climb inside. After a pause of exquisite duration—about enough time to draw a long breath—a man dived headfirst out the tiny side window of the camper. He landed rolling, came up running, and headed straight for our camp in impressive bounding strides. He was wearing nothing but a red union suit, and I remember thinking I had to get one just like it.

The one-piece construction of a union suit seals in body heat and prevents those back-chilling gaps that occur when you bend over while wearing two-piece underwear. The idea's been around at least since the cowboy days of the nineteenth century, though the origin of the name "union suit" remains veiled in mystery. It might refer to the unifying of a top with a bottom, or perhaps to the labor unions that organized the textile industry in the late nineteenth century. A garment similar to our "long johns" was worn in the ring by John L. Sullivan, the bare-knuckles boxer of the 1880s and 1890s, but the name goes back farther, to 1840, when a German exercise guru named Friederich Ludwig Jahn became the father of modern gymnastics by inventing horizontal and parallel bars, balance beams, and side horses. Jahn also designed a full-body workout costume that became the rage of gymnasts all over the world. It didn't take long for "long Jahns" to become "long johns."

With Duofold's patenting in 1906 of two-layer insulated underwear, the traditional wool union suit was transformed forever. Wool has long been a favorite choice of fabrics for people who spend much time outside in cold weather, but if you've ever worn a scratchy wool shirt against bare skin you can sympathize with old-timers who were reluctant to put on a fresh one. The Duofold system worked so well it's still around. The union suit I wore those cold nights in October has an outer layer of 40 percent wool, 50 percent cotton, and 10 percent nylon, covering an inner layer of 100 percent cotton. The combination is warm and easy on the skin, and still contains enough wool to qualify as a classic and to insulate in the event of a soaking.

Not everyone is as enthusiastic as I am. Critics of one-piece long underwear note that they're inconvenient to wash, are a haven for ticks and fleas, and if you get your legs wet wading a stream, they force you to strip from head to toe to dry. A less delicate matter involves bodily functions. It requires an adventurous spirit to negotiate a union suit's famous buttoned seat while squatting against a tree. And there's also the real possibility that the efficient insulation of a union suit will make it *too* warm for many outdoor activities.

Personally, I'm willing to accept the disadvantages. If I expect to work up a sweat I wear polypropylene underwear. But if the weather's cold and I plan mostly sedate activities like trolling in Lake Michigan, drifting slowly downstream in a canoe, or hunting in a blind, I prefer the union suit. Red, of course—the color of emergencies. I don't look for trouble, but if trouble should come lumbering after me some night when I'm half-dressed I plan to land running, with the same style and grace as that guy in Yellowstone.

Good Company

IF YOU WANT YOUR COMPANIONS WITH YOU FOR THE long haul, without shortcuts or easy intimacies, you'll probably agree with Aristotle that friendship is a slow-ripening fruit. It's fine to go canoeing with new acquaintances, but paddling all day with the wrong partner can make the fruit get ripe real fast. It can go all the way to rotten in no time at all.

I've been lucky in love and friendship and have had the good fortune to pass many days and nights in beautiful places with people who challenge and educate and inspire me. I'll always remember the gentle adjustments to each of my favorite partners—how after a day or two most of the routine decisions are made with a raised eyebrow, a nod, a questioning syllable and an answering grunt. Real conversation comes most often in the evening, beside the fire or in the tent, when what is said is said from the heart with words that can bond people for life. A paddling partner is a team member, and naturally you want to team up with someone who is considerate, thoughtful, hardworking, dependable—who values the team over the individual. I'm grateful for the time I've spent

on the water with Craig Date, Mark Wilkes, Mike Mc-
Cumby, my wife, Gail, and my sons, Aaron and Nick. But
I've also endured my share of unfortunate pairings. Trust me:
You want to avoid getting in a boat with a guy who lobs cans
of beer at passing canoes and makes grenade sounds when
they strike the water.

Canoes are simply too small to accommodate clashing
personalities. It's why solo boats are so popular and why you
should never carry guns, machetes, chainsaws, ball-peen ham-
mers, or tincture of cyanide on tandem trips of more than a
few hours' duration. Even a good friendship can be tested by
the rigors of living out of a seventeen-foot watercraft. In the
great tradition of paddling with companions, it's important
that a few observations be made.

For some reason, spouses make poor partners. This is not
universally true, of course, but husbands tend to view paddling with their wives as a challenge on the order of repairing
major appliances, pouring cement driveways, and felling giant
oaks. A husband often ends a Sunday float trip shouting at his
wife while she sits motionless in the bow seat, absolutely mute
with rage. I've seen it a dozen times. He bellows "Turn right!
Turn right! Turn right! Goddammit!" while at the same time
steering with tremendous plunging strokes of his paddle
straight into the fallen tree on the left.

Unless you're an evangelist yourself, you should probably
shy away from entering canoes with anyone who displays
evangelical fervor for philosophy, religion, or politics. Try to
be tolerant of others' opinions, but remember that once on
the water you're a captive audience.

It's generally best to avoid companions who insist on
claiming the stern seat; who announce, "I think I used to do
this a lot when I was in college"; who view the outdoors
as the proper setting for fraternity cheers, yodeling, boom

boxes, or the launching of fireworks; who think children do not belong on canoe trips; who exhibit large doses of competitive zeal; who never stop talking; who turn sullen or disappear when it's time to portage, build a fire, set up a tent, or wash the dishes; who are not humbled by the sight of a clear sky at night; who are more interested in Budweiser than loons.

The quickest way to get to know people is to spend a few days with them. You can do it by getting together over coffee or a beer and chatting, but the process is speeded dramatically by rolling up your sleeves and going to work. The type of work hardly matters—cutting firewood, driving nails, paddling a canoe across a big lake in the wind. It's the effort that reveals character. Years ago, when my brother-in-law, Tim Roth, and I were getting acquainted, we set off for a long weekend of canoeing and fishing at a place I knew in Ontario. We had already spent a few weeks building houses together, so I was relatively sure Tim would be good company. But you never know.

We drove to Canada on a Thursday afternoon and along the way heard the weather forecast on the radio. It was not encouraging. A cold front moving down from the north was expected to bring some rain. We got to the lake early in the evening and crossed it before the storm hit, paddling into a breeze already lifting whitecaps. After portaging a small falls at the upper end of the lake, we paddled a few miles upstream on a low, sluggish tributary lined with lily pads and cattails. The sky by then was low, dark, and sullen. The wind carried bitter spits of rain.

We camped on a patio-size slab of granite beside a short rapids linking two ponds. We set up my pup tent just as the rain began. There was no time to cook dinner.

I've fished in the rain many times, often with great success. It doesn't bother me. Tim and I had brought rain gear and were motivated by a driving urge to catch pike and brook trout.

But this was not a normal rainstorm. A normal rainstorm falters occasionally. It has boundaries. It has a beginning, a middle, and an end. This rainstorm seemed determined never to end. It started as a downpour and it continued as a downpour. It was a gully washer, a ground pounder, a blitzkrieg. It was biblical in its intensity. It fell with such force that it raised a fog of spray over the rocks around us and shattered the surface of the lake to chaos. Thunder tumbled across the sky. Lightning strobed the woods.

We crawled into our sleeping bags at barely eight o'clock, made a dinner of peanut-butter sandwiches, and enjoyed the novelty of being tentbound. We felt lucky to be out of the rain, thankful we were not still on the water looking for a campsite. It was snug and secure in the tiny nylon structure, and we were two friends who were glad we had married sisters. We were sure that in the morning we would wake to blue sky.

But the rain did not stop. It went on all night in undiminished fury. By morning capillaries of water ran down the nylon above our faces, gathered at the seams where they joined the floor, and flowed to the downhill end of the tent, where they formed a pool at our feet. Every half hour or so we unzipped the tent long enough to bail it out with our coffee cups. As hard as we tried, we could not keep the bottoms of our sleeping bags out of the water.

All day the rain pounded the earth. It was relentless. It was like watching a temper tantrum go on for eighteen hours. By evening, we decided, the rain would have to slow. If it diminished even by half we could put on our rain gear and go fishing.

I, who seldom travel without books, had decided to be sensible and bring nothing to read because I did not want to carry the extra weight. Besides, I knew I would spend every spare moment fishing. But not in this rain. I tried, briefly, in the afternoon. The rain drove into me with such force that it found leaks everywhere in my rain jacket. I could feel the water running down my shoulders and under my arms. My reel made sickly screeching noises when I pulled line from it. The lake had risen noticeably and turned the color of chocolate milk. Even before I made the first cast I knew that every fish was hunkered down somewhere on the bottom, as miserable as I was. In fifteen minutes I was back in the tent, drenched now, stripping out of my soaked clothing and settling into my sleeping bag for the duration of the storm. I would have gladly paid twenty dollars for a tattered paperback.

Tim had brought a cop novel by Joseph Wambaugh. He pulled it from his backpack with a flourish and a grin, as if it were a chocolate cake. He read the first page, tore it carefully from the book, and handed it to me.

With care I made every sentence last ten or twenty seconds, every paragraph a minute or two. I reread phrases lovingly. I went back to the top and scanned with careful attention to be sure I had missed nothing interesting. When I could wring no more pleasure from the page I crumpled it into a wad and threw it to the bottom of the tent to absorb water. Tim passed me another.

The rain went on, and the book grew slowly thinner. In the evening Tim reached the last page. He read it twice and handed it to me with a sigh. I read it twice myself, savoring every sentence, and tossed it to the floor. The entire book was there, a heap of fist-size, soggy balls. We gathered them and dumped them outside, ridding the tent of a gallon of water.

When there was nothing left to read, we talked. We told each other our life stories. We shared intimate memories of girlfriends, funny stories from childhood, every stupid and unlucky thing we had ever done. The rain did not stop; neither did our conversation. We slept when we got tired, woke when we were rested, and told stories to pass the time. We talked much of the night Friday, all day Saturday, and late into Saturday night. By the end of the weekend all our possessions were soaked with rain, and we knew each other exceedingly well.

Sunday came, and still the rain did not stop. We broke camp in the rain, loaded the canoe in the rain, paddled all day to the car in the rain. And here's the amazing part: We ended the trip laughing, still friends. We've remained friends to this day.

Good paddling companions don't come along every day, and you can't always recognize them right away. My advice is to paddle mostly with friends, good friends, those with whom you've signed blood oaths as children or built houses or climbed mountains or survived epic downpours. Life is short. Share it with people you like.

The Mysterious Thermos

ONE WAY TO STAY WARM IN THE WINTER IS FROM THE inside, with the hot beverage of your choice. But unless you're willing to boil a billy every time you want a cup of tea, you better bring along a thermos. Make that Thermos, with a capital T—the folks who own the company have always been touchy on the subject of trade names.

I'm a second-generation Thermos man, having received my first bottle many years ago as a gift from my father. I was a greenhorn construction worker at the time, the youngest guy on a crew hired to frame houses that winter. When I described to Dad how I spent my days crawling along icy rafters trying to drive sixteen-penny nails while wearing mittens, he took pity on me and gave me his best old Thermos: a battered, bullet-shaped, steel affair that was as ugly as an old boot but sturdy enough to prop up a Sherman tank. It dated back to the Korean War, which is not particularly old by Thermos standards. The company itself started in 1907.

The first day with my new old Thermos, while I bent happily over a cup of hot coffee during morning break, one of the resident comedians kept me distracted with the old riddle about the intelligence of the Thermos bottle—"It can keep hot drinks hot and cold drinks cold, but how does it know the difference?"—while his buddy spiked my nail apron to the floor. We were always doing things like that. Life on the construction crew was a laugh a minute. Later that day somebody bumped my Thermos, and it rolled off the floor and fell into the driveway, where a lumber truck backed over it. No problem. Didn't hurt it a bit.

If you're on a fishing, hunting, or canoeing expedition where it's important to minimize the weight and bulk of your equipment, a Thermos is one of those nonessentials that can easily be left behind. But for casual trips in cold weather it's always a welcome addition. Sipping a cup of coffee or tea while drifting down a river satisfies the basic need for comfort food. There's also a kind of poetry involved when the steam rising from your cup blends with the mist hanging over a winter-shrouded river. It makes a nice picture.

Thermos is a brand name, but long use and high exposure have transformed it, like Kleenex and Band-Aids, into a generic noun. There are other companies that make good vacuum-sealed bottles (I've had decent luck with a Uno-Vac, for instance, and I'm told that Nissan, of all companies, makes a good one), and the only reason I remain loyal to the Thermos company is that theirs was the first one I owned and it kept me faithful company through some hard years. That's not to say all their products are flawless. The steel models are as sturdy as cast-iron piping, but don't waste your money on the glass-lined plastic ones. If you tip them over or drop them, the liners break with a sickening shudder.

On the job site, where durability really matters, the veterans all use modified Thermoses. Some attach leather handles with hose clamps. Others decorate their bottles with paint and colored tape for easy identification at break time, when every minute counts. Everyone keeps old bottles until they're so battered the tops no longer fit.

Veteran Thermos users also have a few tricks up their sleeves to improve performance. Beverages will stay hot longer, for instance, if you first fill the bottle with boiling water to preheat the inside. Let it sit for a few minutes, then dump the water and refill with your hot beverage. That way you'll have hot coffee all morning and tepid coffee until late in the afternoon. And of course you can precool a Thermos to keep cold beverages colder, making it equally useful in all seasons and climates.

So, how *does* it know?

Dumb Moves

I LIKE TO THINK I'VE LEARNED A THING OR TWO DURING my stay on this planet, but the evidence does not always prove it. When I was seventeen, Doug Shaw and I drove his father's lovingly maintained pickup truck to a nearby lake to go fishing. "Be careful with the truck," we were told, with powerful emphasis, as we backed from the driveway. Doug drove as if the truck were made of porcelain. It took us forty-five minutes to travel fifteen miles.

At the lake we backed down the incline at the boat ramp to the edge of the water. Doug left the engine running, shifted the transmission to neutral, and set the emergency brake. As we stepped out to unload the boat, the brake slipped. The truck rolled backward into the lake, floated to the edge of the drop-off, and sank. When it reached bottom nothing remained above water but the top of the cab and the nose of the hood. We climbed on the hood and cast for trout while waiting for the wrecker to arrive. I remember being surprised at how long it took for the little bubbles to stop trailing up from the submerged gas tank cap. I remember being surprised, too, that Doug's dad eventually forgave us.

Errors of youth hardly count, of course. They're un-avoidable and inevitable and hardly unexpected. I can prob-ably be forgiven for setting off at the age of twenty with Mike McCumby on a March canoe trip on a river swollen over the banks with snowmelt and carrying entire trees in its flow. After lunch we capsized, were dragged underwater by heavy clothes (we did not wear personal flotation devices in those days), made it to the shore, where we set off jogging down a logging trail looking for help, and were probably dangerously hypothermic when we stumbled upon a man and his son, who took us home, dried our clothes, and fed us hot soup. We found the canoe later that day, but never recovered most of our camping and fishing gear.

THE TROUBLE WITH dumb moves is that they come back to haunt you. On a canoe trip with Craig Date a decade ago on the Rifle River in Michigan, I supervised the loading of the canoe. I saw to it that every piece of equipment was secured and waterproofed and placed in such a way as to balance the load: extra canoe paddles here, fishing tackle there, sleeping bags and spare clothes wrapped in plastic bags and secured just so in the duffels. I was such a pain in the neck that Craig finally threw up his hands and announced, "*You* load the boat," and walked off to explore the shoreline. That evening, eight miles downstream, we discovered that I had forgotten to load the pack containing the cooking kit, plates, and bowls. Also the food. I announced that there was nothing to worry about and set out to catch a mess of trout. After two hours I managed to land a single seven-inch rainbow. For dinner we toasted the trout on a forked stick until its flesh was flaky and charred a lovely black. When I tried to remove it from the stick, Craig's share fell into the fire.

Sometimes, if we're lucky, we have the pleasure of witnessing some deserving fool's dumb move. I'm thinking of the powerboater who rode circles around my canoe one afternoon, throwing up conflicting wakes that left me shouting in fury and battling to stay upright. After a few minutes of the fun, he sped off laughing. He accelerated to full throttle and had gone perhaps fifty yards when he struck a submerged sandbar. The impact tore something vital from the lower unit of his motor. He was drifting helplessly toward the far shore when I paddled past.

Unfortunately, not all of our stupidities are so harmless. Early one winter, while ice-fishing near home on Long Lake, my father and I spotted a skier crossing the freshly frozen lake toward an expanse of ice that we knew two days earlier had been open water. We tried to shout a warning, but the skier could not hear us over the sound of his skis on the ice. As we watched, he broke through, his skis folding like wings beneath him, and he fell into four feet of water. He was lucky. If the ice had held a few moments longer he would have crossed the drop-off into twenty-foot depths.

But he wasn't out of trouble yet. Instead of pushing himself up onto the ice on his belly, distributing his weight evenly, he kept trying to climb up on his knees, pushing his skis and poles ahead of him. The ice broke whenever he put his weight on it. Worse, his floundering was taking him toward deep water. He panicked and began thrashing wildly and shouting for help.

While I ran up the hill to the house for a rope, my father walked out as far on the ice as he dared and got the skier's attention. He persuaded him to abandon his skis and poles, turn back toward shallow water, and slide up on the ice on his belly. By the time I reached the lake with a rope and a long pole, the skier was crawling across the ice toward my father. In a few minutes we had him warming in my car. He was very quiet during the ride home. It should have been the end of the story.

But it wasn't. Falling through the ice is a dumb move, but it could happen to anyone. Lakes sometimes freeze in uneven patterns, and unless you're familiar with the water and have followed the weather closely, it can be easy to assume the entire lake is safe. Even thrashing around in panic is understandable in water a degree or two warmer than freezing. It can be forgiven.

What can't be forgiven was our wet skier's ultimate dumb move the next day, when he showed up at the lake carrying a coil of rope and accompanied by his five-year-old daughter. My father intercepted the pair on their march toward yesterday's fractured ice.

"I'm getting my skis," the fellow said, anticipating my father's obvious question.

Dad, eyeing the rope and the five-year-old, the glimmering of a dreadful idea rising within him, asked, "How do you propose to do that?"

"I'm going to tie this rope around my daughter's waist and have her walk out there—"

"Stop."

"She can grab the skis—"

"Stop."

"She only weighs forty pounds—"

"Stop. You are not sending that child out on the ice!"

"But those skis cost me two hundred bucks!"

"I understand that. Go to shore. Leave the skis. They'll still be there when the ice is safe. And if they're not, believe me, two hundred dollars is a very small price to pay."

Smoke Gets in Your Eyes

A CAMPFIRE IS ONLY AS GOOD AS THE WOOD IT IS BUILT with, an easy truth learned the hard way by many a camper hunched hungry and cold over a smoking pile of basswood. If you appreciate a good campfire—better yet, if you appreciate the difference between a good campfire and a great campfire—you're probably a connoisseur of wood and a fastidious builder of woodpiles. Our breed could live by the credo "Not Just Any Stick Will Do."

Camping manuals often recommend packing those dinky folding camp saws, some of which have nothing more than a length of serrated wire for a blade. The implication is that cutting wood on a camping trip is no big deal and you might not want to bother bringing a saw at all. Sure, you can break enough wood over your knee to get by, if all you want from a fire is enough heat to warm your Spam and maybe smoke-dry a pair of socks. But if you're after more than mere utility you flat-out need a decent saw and an ax.

Substandard woodcutting implements are not only frustrating, they're dangerous. One of the first things you learn in Boy Scouts is that if you must use a hatchet, never swing it freely to chop wood. Instead, cut a mallet—a two-foot length of branch the diameter of a rolling pin or baseball bat—and use the mallet to drive the head of the hatchet like a splitting wedge. Better yet, use an ax. An ax can have a shortened handle for convenient transport, but it should be hefty enough to prevent it from glancing off a chunk of firewood—the most common cause of ax and hatchet accidents. Likewise, don't waste your money on a flimsy camp saw. Spend the extra ten or twenty bucks for a good one like the Schmidt Packsaw, which is made in Maine of red oak, folds into a compact, safe package, and can cut logs up to a foot in diameter. Thus armed, you can get on with the important business of cutting and stacking wood.

I like building woodpiles, enjoy their suggestion of industry and readiness and the aura of permanence they lend to a campsite. When I make camp, even a quick camp I know will last only until the next morning, the first thing I do after putting up the tent is get to work on the woodpile. Thoreau's famous dictum that his fire warmed him twice suggests the great holistic truth of open fires. The pleasure is much greater than the flame itself. It starts with the cutting, carrying, splitting, and stacking of the wood, and it continues through every stage of building, lighting, and feeding the fire. It doesn't end until the last orange coal winks out in its bed of ashes.

The reason thousands of homeowners prefer real fireplaces to gas imitations should be obvious. An open fire appeals to all the senses. The crack of exploding resin, the enthusiastic whoop of flame sucking oxygen, the thump of a log settling into coals are sounds we learn to associate with contentment and well-being. A fire sounds good and looks good. It also smells good. If I didn't come home surrounded by a nimbus of campfire scent, I'd think the weekend had been wasted. Woodsmoke flushes tear ducts and perfumes a body with the aroma of the woods. Anyone with a fairly good nose learns the differences among those aromas. You can recognize the bright fragrance of mesquite, the subtle sweetness of cherry, the cloying thickness of balsam and spruce and red cedar.

Everyone seems to have their favorite firewood. Thoreau liked "hard green wood just cut" because it burned long enough to be waiting in his cabin when he came home after walking for hours. Sigurd Olson gathered old pine knots that had lain for years under pine needles, preserved by the heavy resin impregnated in their grains, and considered burning them a spiritual event. Edward Abbey gathered desert juniper for his "squaw" fire and declared it "the sweetest fragrance on the face of the earth. . . . I doubt if all the smoking censers of Dante's paradise could equal it."

Aldo Leopold insisted that mesquite, that ubiquitous shrub of the Southwest, was the best of fragrant fuels. "Brittle with a hundred frosts and floods," he wrote in *A Sand County Almanac,* "baked by a thousand suns, the gnarled imperishable bones of these ancient trees lie ready-to-hand at every camp, ready to slant blue smoke across the twilight, sing a song of teapots, bake a loaf, brown a kettle of quail, and warm the shins of man and beast."

In the upland forests of the Great Lakes region, our campfire wood of choice is dead maple, air-dried on the stump. We look for saplings a few inches in diameter that died young in the battle for sunlight and space, crowded out by bigger, more robust trees. They're found in every stand of hardwoods, in the shade of every grandfather maple, sometimes dying in thickets dense as cane brakes. Long after they lose their leaves, branches, and bark, the dead saplings remain upright, bone dry, brittle, and clean, like ancient lances. They can be brought down with a push, dragged to camp, and sawed into lengths. They split easily into kindling, or, burned in the round, roar with flame and heat, creating a fire that burns for hours, sends a trail of fragrant smoke wisping through the woods, and builds a bed of coals that lasts the night. Those small logs of maple can be stacked so neatly that there's a tendency to construct woodpiles that will live on long after you've left a camp.

THERE'S AN ART to building a fire, and those who get good at it tend to become intolerant of techniques other than their own. The first time Kelly Galloup and I camped together, on a stretch of trout river in Michigan, we circled each other warily, each certain the other would put together a less-than-perfect fire. It was raining—had been all day—and the fire demanded special attention. We went in opposite directions looking for wood. Both of us sought old pine, the remnant stumps of white and red pines cleared in the turn-of-the-century logging frenzy that decimated the old forests of Michigan. Kelly got back to camp before me and whittled the wet wood away from the dry, resin-soaked heart of the pine and placed it at the center of a teepee of maple and cedar. I was relieved to see that he knew what he was doing.

The secret is patience and oxygen. The more adverse the conditions—the wetter the woods and the scarcer the fuel—the more important it is to take your time. Kindling must be dry and abundant, larger wood stacked at hand and ready to apply one stick at a time. The foundation of a fire is built on a carefully assembled structure of dry tinder. It must be solid enough to resist falling apart but spacious enough to allow air to circulate to the flames. A hundred camp manuals suggest a hundred techniques, but nothing teaches better than trial and error.

Where there's fire, of course, there's smoke. When we were children my friends and I were convinced that saying the phrase "I hate rabbits" would cause pesky smoke to shift away from us. The habit stuck. We're adults now, too often distracted by adult problems, but when we sit around a camp-fire together, sipping drinks, eating, talking, we still squint and lean back as the smoke turns in our direction, and, without thinking, say, "Rabbits."

The fire is the heart of a camp. It connects us with a hundred generations of fire watchers, making us part of a tradition so ancient and elemental it has no name. A fire initiates conversation, breaks social ice, gives comfort and satisfaction. It's especially satisfying when you can watch it change your old friends into kids again.

Camp Coffee

MORNING SIMPLY ISN'T MORNING WITHOUT A CUP OF coffee, but not just any cup will do. I want mine freshly brewed with clean cold water and served in a ceramic mug of substance—not a plastic cup and, please, not one of Styrofoam—and I want it black and strong enough to kick-start me into wakefulness.

It's no accident, I think, that a cup of coffee is approximately the size and temperature of a human heart. Though it does not beat with life, it steams and radiates and arouses the senses with its aroma, its flavor, its warmth. We hunch over it seeking comfort and affirmation, our hands clasping it to absorb the heat. It's a poor substitute for love, grace, talent, and good looks, but a hot cup of coffee is a satisfying thing to hold on to early in the morning, while the chill of night remains in your bones and you're not yet ready to face the responsibilities of daytime.

Coffee is such a common ingredient of our daily routines that it's hard to imagine life without it. Yet until the seventeenth century it was unknown in Europe and confined only to northern Africa and the Arab world. The coffee plant was found originally only in Ethiopia, and our word for it comes from the Turkish, *kahve,* and the Arabic, *qahwah.* When traders brought the brew to Europe, Christians were wary of its stimulatory qualities and declared it an invention of the devil. Then Pope Clement VIII tried a cup and liked the brew so much that he baptized it, and the Western world has been on a caffeine jag ever since.

No doubt coffee was brewed outside over open fires for centuries before it found its way into the posh coffeehouses of Vienna and Paris. Indoors or out, it can be percolated, drip brewed, steamed, slow filtered—there are many ways to make it, and you're wise to remain open to procedures ancient and new. Years ago I learned one method for brewing from an ancient, shrunken man who had spent most of his life working as a timber cutter in the Upper Peninsula of Michigan. One morning I stopped by to visit and watched him fill a fire-blackened pot with water and set it on a grill over an open fire in the yard. The moment the water reached the boiling point, he scooped a generous handful of Maxwell House from a can, threw it in the pot, and slammed the lid over it. In a few moments the pot trembled, the lid rattled loose, and liquid and grounds spilled over the sides into the fire, giving off steaming clouds of aroma. Using his slouch hat for a pot holder, he lifted the pot off the fire and dropped a broken eggshell inside to settle the grounds. I accepted a cup with doubts. It was as thick and dark as silt at the bottom of a pond. I took a tentative sip, expecting my stomach to clench against the bitterness. But it was good. Delicious, in fact. I had several cups.

The experts say bitter flavor is usually the result of too much boiling, which releases tannin and makes the coffee acidic. To avoid bitterness in a percolator, remove it from the fire a minute or two after it starts to boil, then pour a tablespoon of cold water down the spout to clear the grounds. Better yet, use the below-boiling method: Bring water to the boiling point, remove it from the fire to cool for a few moments, then pour it over ground coffee in a filtered drip pot.

Connoisseurs might choose to bring along a portable coffee grinder (on the market now is a backpacker's model that weighs just five ounces and fits in a shirt pocket) and an espresso maker for use on a camp stove. The one I've seen weighs seven ounces and can make a three-ounce cuplet of espresso in ninety seconds. With a bag of roasted Kona Kai beans and a pint of cream you can whip up a brew that makes you think you're back home in your neighborhood Starbucks.

But you don't need to be that fussy. Outdoors, on a cold morning, even a pretty bad cup of coffee tastes pretty good. Tom Carney and I once spent two days riding horses through the North Dakota badlands in the company of a pair of cowboys. They were the genuine article, bow legged and tobacco chewing, raised on cattle ranches as big as counties, where they had learned the cowboy skills of horsemanship, fence mending, cattle branding, and, of course, coffee making. At night we slept on the ground beneath the stars, and in the morning woke to the scent of frying bacon and eggs. Tom and I got out of our sleeping bags, groaning with aching muscles, and went looking for coffee. One of the cowboys handed us Styrofoam cups, plastic spoons, and a small jar of instant Folgers, then pointed at a pot of water simmering on the camp stove. When we hesitated, the cowboy took a noisy slurp from his own Styrofoam cup, squinted at us through the steam, and said, in a voice that sounded as if it had been dragged all night behind a horse, "Now *that,* mister, is a damned good cup of coffee."

I stirred up a cup and tried a sip. It wasn't Jamaica Blue Mountain, but it wasn't bad. Not bad at all.

Tumplines

YEARS AGO, ON A PORTAGE TRAIL IN ONTARIO, I MET AN apparition. It emerged molecule by molecule from a valley pooled with fog, climbed toward me in silence, and finally took the shape of a stocky young man wearing ragged jeans and a flannel shirt. But something was wrong with him. He staggered instead of walked, and his head seemed to be harnessed to his shoulders as if in traction for a neck injury. Without even a nod of greeting he detoured off the trail to let me pass. On his back was a pack big enough to carry a circus tent. Of course. This was no ghost with back problems. It was an ordinary guy using a tumpline.

Tumplines are found in cultures from the Amazon to the Arctic and are probably as ancient as flint fire starters and stone axes. In their simplest forms they're strips of leather or lengths of rope hung from the head to support a load. Sounds inelegant, and it is, but a load suspended from a tump causes the spine to straighten and the weight to be distributed from the long bones and powerful muscles of the thighs all the way up the back and neck. By some accounts a tumpline allows you to carry an extra twenty-five pounds with no increase in effort.

A scan of the literature reveals some ambivalence about the device, however. Horace Kephart wrote in *Camping and Woodcraft* that a tump is "a good addition not only to a pack harness but to almost any other kind of pack used for carrying heavy weights. Generally it will not be used until the shoulders tire; then it relieves the strain. It is an advantage in climbing steep hillsides." John J. Rowlands called the tumpline "One piece of gear I couldn't get along without. . . . Don't know who invented it, but it is about the handiest thing you can have on the trail. . . . With a tumpline you can carry a load of firewood as easily as you can a blanket roll or pack. . . . You can't afford to be without one."

Bill Riviere thinks otherwise. In *The L. L. Bean Guide to the Outdoors* he states emphatically that "The tumpline, unless you're toughened to it, is an instrument of torture and it has virtually disappeared." Calvin Rutstrum, in *North American Canoe Country,* admits that "Some people find difficulty in using the tumpline," probably because they have "weak neck muscles."

The more usual cause of difficulty with a tumpline is improper adjustment. For it to work, the strap must fit just right, the traces must be the right length to place the load against the center of your back, and you must lean forward at the proper angle against the load. There is a very small margin of error. If the adjustments are off by as little as two inches, you lose the benefits of the tump and might as well carry everything on your shoulders.

A tump can also be fitted to a portage yoke to help ease the strain of carrying a canoe. Bill Mason devised a serviceable one of leather that he strapped to a pair of paddles when he used them as a yoke, but as he pointed out in *Path of the Paddle,* "the tumpline must be adjusted perfectly or it's agony." Cliff Jacobson recommends a simple and useful system in his *The New Wilderness Canoeing and Camping*. It utilizes elastic straps and a square of canvas, and has the advantage of not slipping off your forehead every time you take a lurching step and the canoe bounces.

I was more curious than convinced the first time I tried a tumpline on a backpack. The portage was less than a half mile, and the pack weighed only forty pounds, but since a tumpline came as a standard accessory on the pack I decided to put it to use. It took a few minutes to adjust the straps (and each adjustment required taking the pack off and putting it on again), and I learned quickly that the headstrap must be worn slightly above the forehead, not on it. Once it was fitted and adjusted, however, much of the load was taken off my shoulders and lower back, and I no longer suffered the usual strap aches. Maybe it was psychological, like grunting, but it seemed to help when the going got tough.

The discovery put a new bounce to my step. I trekked up hills with gusto and rounded curves like a bicyclist on banked turns. The strap kept my head anchored in place, so when I wanted to look around I had to turn my entire torso, and when I met a pair of hikers coming toward me on the trail I couldn't nod as I passed. I smiled, but with the strain on my neck muscles it may have come across as a grimace. Looks of faint horror showed on their faces. I tried to signal with my eyebrows to tell them that everything was fine, but they were hurrying away by then and I don't think they got the message.

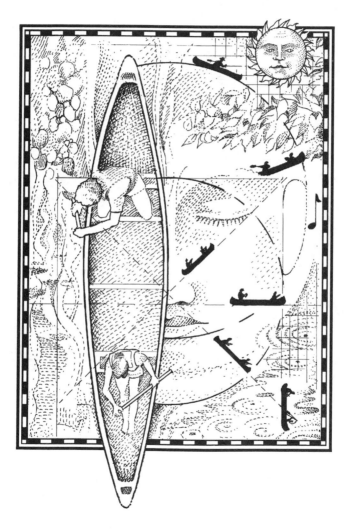

CANOEING AND KAYAKING HAVE BECOME SO POPULAR that on some rivers it is almost impossible to find water you can call your own. That fact has unhappy implications for those of us who got into the sport as a way to find places nobody else knows about. But face it: You can't keep a good thing to yourself. On any better-than-average American river on a summer weekend, you'd better plan on sharing.

We tend to think of crowded water as a recent phenomenon, but for several decades in the late nineteenth and early twentieth centuries, canoeing in wood-and-canvas boats was a tremendously popular social activity. The image of the lone wilderness paddler had romantic appeal but was clearly not something most urban dwellers wanted to experience. Judging by old photos of nattily dressed canoeists cramming the water around Belle Isle in Detroit, the Charles River in Boston, Central Park in New York City, and other capitals of pre-Great-Depression culture, canoeing was a great way to meet people, find relief from summer heat, and have good clean fun in a healthy environment.

Those are still fine reasons to get out paddling, though I

admit this with reservations. When rivers and lakes become too popular, they suffer from litter, erosion, and habitat destruction. It's the usual story. Many of my fly-fishing friends, who are not gracious about sharing the water, harbor a grudge against paddlers and refer to the weekend crowds as the "aluminum hatch." It's an apt name, especially on rivers that support thriving commercial canoeing industries. Some liveries fill the rivers by promoting a theme-park canoeing experience. In the mornings livery employees dump dozens of aluminum canoes beside the river, fill them with people who have never canoed before, and push them out into the current. The people, because they are in an unfamiliar environment, cling together for security, rather the way you would cling to fellow passengers if your ship were going down during a transatlantic crossing. After a while the livery employees haul their trailers a few miles downstream and wait for clusters of canoes to show up. Sometimes the canoes arrive without the people, and sometimes the people arrive without the canoes. Or the canoes and people arrive together, but the canoes are dented and swamped, and the people are wet, sunburned, and exhausted. The livery employees arrange the canoeists in line, charge them extra for broken and lost equipment, and then drive them away to make room for the next batch of customers.

The crazy thing is, it can be fun. This reaction seems to contradict my nature. I usually try hard to avoid people when I'm canoeing and fishing, but there are days when I enjoy elbowing into a crowd of cheerful, boisterous paddlers. I'll even accept a cold drink when it's offered, or when I find one bobbing in the water. After years of experience I can always spot full cans of beer and soda as they ride downstream in a river. Like icebergs, they float seven-eighths submerged. Empties and broken Styrofoam coolers collect in the eddies and logjams, but it's encouraging to note that more and more commercial liveries routinely organize river cleanups at the end of the season. I'm also encouraged by how many paddlers understand basic river etiquette. Most know enough to give anglers a wide berth, and if every damned one of them asks "Ketchinany?" at least they ask with warm intentions. Even on the most crowded water, good fellowship abounds.

People are constantly demonstrating that human nature is as variable, refreshing, and unanticipated as anything in the natural world. Just when you're stoked up from watching an osprey snatch a trout from the river or a black bear bawling at her cub on the bank, you see a naked fat guy in a canoe wearing a lampshade on his head. Or you come around a bend and see a man hanging from the limb of a low-hanging tree with his hands, while clinging to the stern of his canoe with his feet—stretched like a blasphemer on the rack—and his wife and kids are kneeling in the bottom of the canoe laughing so hard they're in danger of capsizing. Or some un-expectedly cold Fourth of July you meet a pair of college kids on the river warming their hands over a bonfire blazing in the middle of their aluminum Grumman.

One summer day my friend Craig Date and I paddled around a wide bend in the Muskegon River and found three young ladies standing in a line in water up to their waists. Their clothes lay plastered to their skin, their wet hair hung in their faces. When they saw us they started waving and yelling. They had obviously been waiting for someone to come along and rescue them.

"Can you help us get our canoe?" they shouted.

Craig and I looked around. No canoe was in sight. I thought of the power of the Muskegon, and it seemed likely that their boat was swamped and tumbling in the current, perhaps already submarining deep into the backwaters of the next dam downstream. "Where is it?" we asked, already quite sure they would never see their canoe again.

"We're *in* it!" the three girls shouted. "We're *standing* in it!"

I do most of my serious paddling and fishing Monday through Friday, when I can count on having water to myself. On weekends my favorite rivers are crowded with bevies of rental canoes and bank-to-bank rafts of inner tubes stuffed with grinning river enthusiasts. I can live with that. If I go out on a Saturday or Sunday it is to mix with people, to have fun, to share a favorite place with kindred spirits. These are crowded times, sure, but it's good to know that some crowds are better than others.

Praiseworthy Paddles

WHEN IT COMES TO TECHNOLOGY, MANY OF US HAVE mixed feelings. We tend to hate it almost as much as we love it. Even while we blame it for the mess the world is in, we're waiting for more of it to come along and bail us out. Canoe paddles made of plastic, Kevlar, and graphite might seem like the best things to come along since hermetically sealed beef jerky, but we're convinced that no paddle can compare to an old-fashioned wooden one.

A plastic paddle does the job, but a good wooden one is a pleasure to use. Wood slices the water silently, subtly, without clubbing or splashing. Its qualities become more apparent the more you use it. In the hands of a master, it can perform masterfully.

I have two good paddles on my desk as I write this: a traditional beavertail made of cherry and an ottertail made of black walnut, both manufactured by Grey Owl Paddles of Cambridge, Ontario. Brian Dorfman, owner and managing director of Grey Owl, started the company in 1975, when he was a disenchanted stockbroker who depended on canoeing for mental therapy but was dissatisfied because he couldn't find good wooden paddles he could afford. Taking matters into his own hands, he began a company that now builds some forty to fifty thousand wooden paddles a year, in about twenty-five models. The key to the company's success—and Dorfman's happiness—is the wood. "There's something about the thirty or forty steps that go into a wooden paddle," he says, "that's still fun after all these years. I don't think you could say that about a synthetic paddle manufactured on a machine."

Like bone, wood shrinks and swells with humidity. It breathes the same air we breathe. It adapts after long use to its user, absorbing sweat, growing polished, adjusting to the grip of individual hands. Keep a paddle long enough, treat it with respect, and you end up with an object with character, a possession as personal as a talisman. To someone who cares for it and respects it, a wooden paddle is never merely an incidental accessory to a canoe. In the words of Grey Owl's Brian Dorfman, it becomes more than "just a stick to push a boat along."

One day a few years ago the UPS guy brought me an extraordinary paddle with my name on it. It was a gift from Peter Hitchcock, a craftsman from Snyder, New York, who had contacted me some months earlier with an offer I couldn't refuse. His letter was in the form of a challenge and it was irresistible. "I submit to you," he wrote, "that you presently do not own a wooden paddle. You own a board shaped like a paddle." He promised that if I sent him my height and weight and answered a few questions about my paddling preferences, he would build a custom paddle, "the likes of which you probably have never seen."

The result was a paddle so fine I'm reluctant to use it. Most of the time it stays near at hand in my office, where I can lift it, flex it, admire it whenever I want. Peter gets a bit irritated by that. He insists his paddles are meant to be used, not displayed.

Two remarkable qualities set Hitchcock's paddle above all others I've come across. First is the workmanship. It is so elegant in its simplicity, so light yet strong, so carefully balanced and shaped to my hands that it seems to become an extension of my arms the moment I pick it up. The second quality is its heritage. The design and, more importantly, the techniques for building it were originally practiced by a small group of craftsmen in the Haliburton Highlands and Algonquin Park regions of Ontario, about two hundred miles north of Toronto. Hitchcock became acquainted with four of those paddle makers near the ends of their lives (the last one died in 1971) and learned their secrets. A paddle built by his main mentor in 1931 was in continuous summer use until 1986 and, according to Hitchcock, still looks as good as the day it was made.

The key to these remarkable paddles is the wood—both its quality and the way it is handled. They are made of maple, but not just any maple. Hitchcock considers finding the right tree the biggest challenge to building his paddles. It must be very large, at least two feet in diameter at the trunk, and it must grow in dense, sheltered woods and have no limbs for the first forty or fifty feet of height. The trick is to find a tree, in Hitchcock's words, "that splits perfectly straight for six or seven feet. Even in a hardwood forest full of fine trees this is literally a one-in-a-thousand shot. From the stories I have heard from the old men [from whom he learned] there was only one man in the area who could look at a tree and tell that it would split straight, or, as they would say, 'It was a paddle tree.' They honestly believed these trees 'growed to be made into paddles.' "

Hitchcock gets his trees from a pair of hardwood sawmills

near Buffalo, New York. Occasionally, from the thousands
of maple logs processed, a prime log is set aside to be made
into veneer. When a particularly fine one shows up, a foreman
calls Hitchcock. If he likes what he sees, he buys the log and
immediately splits it lengthwise, using wedges and a maul. If
the log splits straight he splits the halves into quarters, then
takes them to an Amish sawmill, where they are rough-cut
into planks an inch and a half thick.

At this point the lumber differs dramatically from most
used in paddle making. Ordinary boards are "flat sawn" from
a log by running it lengthwise against a circular sawblade,
slicing it into equal widths from the outside in, resulting in
boards with flat grain. Hitchcock's planks are "quarter-sawn,"
cut from the bark to the heart of the log. This is time con-
suming and difficult, because after each cut the single plank
remains and the large remaining piece falls away—just the
opposite of conventional milling—and the large piece must
be set up and adjusted again before each cut. The result is that
the grain of the wood is never crossed during sawing, and the
plank ends up patterned with the tight, striated grain of the
tree.

Each plank is air-dried for a couple of years, then the
general shape of the paddle is cut out with a band saw. Hitchcock has a friend do this, since he owns no power wood-
working machinery. Once he gets the piece back he
submerges it in water for a week to make it easier to work
with and to make sure it does not split or check. All the
remaining work is done entirely by hand with drawknife,
spokeshave, and sandpaper. Each paddle requires about
twenty-five hours of work to carve and make ready for fin-
ishing.

The finish is the most time-consuming process of all, requiring an initial rubdown of linseed oil thinned with mineral

spirits, followed by fifteen to twenty coats of French polish (consisting of equal parts of shellac, linseed oil, and alcohol), and concluding with several coats of marine varnish, sanded and steel-wooled between coats. The finish is allowed to dry for a month, then hand-rubbed first with pumice stone to remove imperfections and finally with rottenstone to bring out the gloss.

The completed paddle is beautiful, the edge-grained wood of the blade a visual record of its parent tree's age and health, the finish rubbed to a deep soft gloss the color of a palomino. It is flexible and incredibly strong. Hitchcock sent me a photo of a 120-pound person sitting on one of his paddles stretched from grip to blade tip between two sawhorses. The paddle bent beneath the weight but did not break. He also sent a crescent-shaped, five-sixteenths-inch slice of wood trimmed from the end of my paddle's blade and challenged me to break it between my hands. It took all my strength.

Paddles made of high-tech materials are efficient and nearly indestructible, but I've not seen one yet that possesses even a hint of the quality found in my paddle built by Hitchcock. In our age of technological wonders, when most of the things we own are standardized, designed to become obsolete, and instantly replaceable, it stands out like a maple in a cornfield. I cherish it as if it were already a family heirloom. It is the paddle of a lifetime.

Shuttle Cars

As a matter of principle I prefer automobiles that are worth less than my canoes. I'm no financial genius, heaven knows, but it seems to make sense to spend money on things that don't plummet in value from one year to the next. Cars depreciate much faster than canoes. Thus it is a shrewd business move to buy a new canoe every few years while driving an old car into the ground. Besides, as every paddler and angler knows, the only really good use for automobiles is to carry you and your gear to the water, and you don't need a showroom BMW for that.

Years ago a friend of mine converted his 1964 Chevy Impala into one of the finest shuttle cars I've ever seen. He yanked the backseat out to make storage room for camping equipment, mounted a compass on the dashboard, and wired a clipboard for maps to the steering wheel. He bolted eye hooks to the bumpers for more convenient rope work, and welded car-top carriers to the roof. Whenever the body showed rust he slapped on a fresh coat of green house paint he had bought on sale at Montgomery Ward. The paint was so bright that when we were still two or three bends away on a river we could see the verdant glow of his car above the trees.

A shuttle car is always immediately recognizable. There are spots on the body where ropes have worn the paint away, gouges on the side panels, a muffler held together with baling wire and fiberglass tape. The inside is so filled with paddles, coolers, personal flotation devices, rods and reels, sleeping bags, and tents that there is scarcely room for a driver, let alone passengers. The tires are bald and the wheels lack hubcaps. The entire car, inside and out, is coated with a uniform layer of good clean dust.

I've owned many decent shuttle cars and trucks, but the best have been station wagons, primarily because of their load capacity. My most recent wagon was a 1980 Ford Fairmont that logged more than 160,000 miles before its final, fatal loss of compression. When packed with care, Old Blue could carry three canoes and six people, all the usual camping and canoeing accessories, plus two or three spare tires and a case of Pennzoil 10W30. She got uncommonly good mileage for a shuttle car—twenty or so miles to the gallon—but leaked a quart of oil every tankful. Also, her front end shimmied at highway speed, she stalled at intersections, and the air-conditioning and the heater both produced about the same volume of lukewarm air. But she took my canoe and me where we wanted to go and usually got us home at the end of the day. You can't ask more than that from a shuttle car.

The great advantage of owning a motor vehicle worth less than a couple of thousand dollars is that it frees you to be gloriously indifferent to the scratches and dents that appear inevitably when you drive rutted back roads in search of rivers. Older vehicles have the further advantage of being much easier to repair than recent models with their complex electronic carburetors and computerized ignition systems. When

you're bucking two-tracks forty miles from the nearest highway, you appreciate a car that can be fixed with a screwdriver,
a crescent wrench, a pair of pliers, and a roll of binding wire.

Marty's brilliant '64 Impala is a case in point. We once
set out in it for Ontario but barely got over the Mackinac
Bridge before the oil-pressure light came on, and the engine
began to buck and cough. We turned from the highway to
a secondary road and pulled over to make repairs. But before
we could even lift the hood we noticed a bridge a hundred
yards ahead of us and strolled over to take a look. It crossed
a river, a beguiling river, with tea-tinted water flowing over
boulders and trout rising methodically in midstream. We
knew we could fix the car—it needed a long drink of oil
and some screwdriver adjustments of its points and distrib-
utor—but it would take an hour, and already the day was
growing short. So we unloaded our gear and set off down
the river. It was the right decision. We had a fine weekend
exploring new territory. The fishing was good and the river
interesting, and we never saw another soul. When we ran
out of time on Sunday we stopped at a bridge, flipped a coin,
and Marty hitchhiked back to the car. He started the engine,
made some minor adjustments, and the car got us home
without incident.

All you really need from a car is dependability. At the end
of a long day on the water, when you're tired, chilled, and
hungry and the sun is gone and the evening turning cool, the
sweetest moment comes when you've put away your gear,
secured your canoe to the carriers, and have settled finally
into the seat of your car. It's dry and comfortable there and
smells like home. You pump the accelerator a few times, take
a deep breath, and turn the key in the ignition. The engine
grinds, coughs, sputters, and catches. It hums, it clatters, it
throws a fine and reassuring spray of lubricant around the

engine compartment. You back around, shift into forward, and lurch down the trail toward the highway. No cowboy ever had a mount so faithful. "Home, Hoss," you say, and she obeys, and all's well with the world.

Let There Be Light

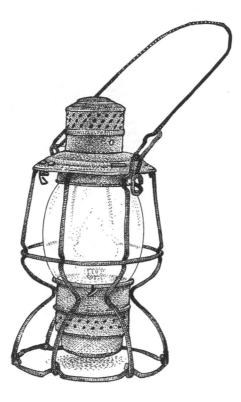

IN THE PERPETUAL QUEST FOR WARMTH AND ILLUMINATION, I prefer campfires, thank you. The dancing light, the heat, the crack of exploding resins, sparks spiraling spaceward like insects in a religious frenzy—what more could you want in the way of heat, light, and companionship? If there is a problem with campfires, it is only that you can't take them into the tent with you, you can't build one without firewood, and they're inconvenient to carry out back to the latrine. The next best thing, I guess, is a Coleman lantern.

If that sounds like a qualified endorsement, it's because Coleman lanterns, while fine for casual camping and fishing trips, are too bulky, heavy, and prone to breakage to be ideal for long-distance expeditions. Tip one over and the mantle—the glowing piece of woven fabric that gives off light—will probably disintegrate into powder. The only time I tried taking a Coleman lantern on a backcountry canoe trip I was plunged into darkness thirty seconds after lighting it and setting it on my beached canoe's seat. While unloading gear, I lurched against the hull, and the lantern fell over. The mantle burst, the lantern wheezed and died, and I was forced to set up my tent by touch. What had seemed like a good idea—a source of dependable, bright light to make camp chores easier—became an annoyance when I had to haul the useless lantern over every portage.

But, aside from their fragile mantles, Coleman lanterns are astonishingly durable. I'm always running into people using chipped and battered models they say are twenty-five or thirty years old. Even dumping one over the side of a canoe won't put it out of business for long. All you need to do is wash out the sand and mud, replace the mantle, pump the gas reservoir, and light the thing. Any parts that can be broken or lost are easily replaced, and no maintenance is required except an occasional drop of oil on the leather washer that seals the pump shaft.

Such durability and simplicity have, for most of this century, put Coleman lanterns high on the list of essential camping gear. William C. Coleman, a schoolteacher and part-time salesman, began making improvements on the gasoline and kerosene lanterns of his day as early as 1902, selling them mostly to farmers and other rural dwellers who were not yet hooked up to electricity. Design improvements led, in 1928, to the Instant-Lite, the basic Coleman most of us know today. If you have any doubt about its success, consider that upwards of fifty million have been sold.

I suspect the secret to the Coleman lantern's popularity is in the illumination itself. The glowing, brilliant white light of a busily hissing Coleman is far more inviting than the static, antiseptic light of a battery-powered lamp or the smelly, dim light of the old kerosene lanterns of our grandparents' day. While it is certainly not as appealing as a good crackling campfire, we gather around it to warm our hands, talk, eat, read, and play cards, and when it's time to sleep we turn the knob that shuts off the gas supply and use those final seconds of residual light while the mantle flickers and dims to climb into our sleeping bags.

Various Coleman lanterns can burn white gas (or, as it is commonly known, "Coleman fuel"), kerosene, propane, or unleaded gasoline. Accessories include tree-trunk hangers, hard-shell and soft-shell carrying cases, directional reflectors, fuel funnels, electronic ignitions, and pads to protect the glass globe during transport and storage.

All that variety is fine, but it's dwarfed in significance by a recent announcement from Coleman headquarters in Wichita, Kansas. According to a company spokesman, a technological breakthrough has produced a new generation of mantles. In appearance they look like the old ones, but they're much tougher and can take considerably more abuse before crumbling to ash. How much abuse can they take? Crash tests under controlled laboratory conditions indicate they can survive a two-foot fall—just about the height of a canoe seat.

I ordered a dozen.

Revenge of the Map

STUDYING MAPS IS A SURE WAY TO MAKE YOURSELF miserable. Those two-dimensional representations of our multidimensional world have a way of igniting wanderlust and overexciting the imagination. Follow the meandering blue line of a river into a sprawling blue maze of lakes and you can easily slip into an idealized version of the place. "I want to be *there*," you whisper. And *there*, and *there*. And when you have finished exploring that irresistible shoreline and climbing that tantalizing promontory, you want to go *there*. Soon you are so exhausted that you can't muster the strength to go anywhere at all.

The best maps for this exercise in futility—and the best for down-and-dirty navigating in the real world—are topographic or quadrant maps. They allow you to see hills and marshes, flat water and rapids, roads and trails and even cabins, and, because they are presented in large-scale formats and blocked off in square-mile grids, they make it possible to tally an accurate mileage count.

Topos also make a genuine effort to illustrate the third dimension. This is accomplished with contour lines, those superimposed jangling lines you see echoing across the page. The more closely the lines are drawn, the steeper the terrain. Likewise, the more frequently the lines cross a river, the steeper its gradient. Counting the contour lines—or, more to the point, counting the intervals between them—makes it possible to measure elevations. If the contour intervals are set at twenty feet, and the map shows ten contour lines crossing a river in ten miles, the total descent for that stretch is two hundred feet, or twenty feet per mile. Such information can be priceless.

With a little practice, you can study a topo map and see the lay of the land—the heights of hills and mountains, the steepness of canyons, the dimensions of swamps and meadows. You can follow the course of a river and determine whether the banks that flank it are two-hundred-footers impossible to climb or two-footers topped by wetlands. You can see at a glance if the river is sluggish or a raging boat eater.

Such details are possible because topo maps are based on aerial photographs. Most of the photos were taken in the 1930s and 1940s, and in the years since have been periodically updated and revised. Revisions, however, are incomplete. The Kiernan, Michigan, quadrangle I just pulled at random from my files is drawn from aerial photos taken in 1944 and field-checked in 1945. New photos were taken in 1955 and again in 1975, but they were never field-checked for errors. Topos might be the best maps we've got, but they're not foolproof.

Craig Date and I learned that lesson one August day on the Brule River on the Michigan-Wisconsin border. In the morning, studying a topo spread on the hood of Craig's truck, we decided to end our trip at a bridge called Scott's Landing. The plan was for our buddy Mark Wilkes to meet us there with the truck at six o'clock and we'd all go to dinner. The day promised to be hot, so Craig and I put on swimsuits, T-shirts, and sneakers. We tossed a quart of water and a couple of apples in the canoe. Mark kept the map.

We spent most of the day drifting lazily with the current and watching wildlife. But as the afternoon ended we became uneasy. We had not kept track of landmarks and had no idea how far we had come. Each time we rounded a bend we expected to see the bridge at Scott's Landing, with Mark standing on it with a bag of sandwiches and a six-pack of beer. But one bend followed another and no bridge appeared. Six o'clock came and went. Then seven o'clock. We began paddling to a racing cadence, trying to beat the sun. Eight o'clock, and still no bridge. Then it got dark.

At first it was easier to keep going than to stop. The Wisconsin shore was dense with cedar swamps, and the Michigan shore rose in a wooded bank a hundred feet high. Even after dark we pushed on, certain the bridge was beyond the next bend. The Brule is not much of a challenge in the daylight, but at night its Class I and II rapids are daunting. We paddled until we could see standing waves only in the periphery of our vision. For a while we navigated by sound more than sight, avoiding the obvious turbulence, seeking channels that Craig, in the bow, would steer us toward. Once we went up on an unseen rock and spun broadside against it. We hung there for a long moment while the river tried to bury our upstream gunwale. Somehow we worked in unison, leaning downstream, applying pry strokes that turned the canoe and let us slide free.

Finally, when it was stupid to continue, we dragged the canoe up the bank and left it on a ledge. Climbing higher, we came to an abandoned railroad bed. The stars gave just enough light to reveal a corridor of darkness running parallel to the river. We built a tripod of dead branches to mark the location of the canoe and began walking in what we hoped was the direction of Scott's Landing.

We walked for hours. It's impossible to know for sure, but it seemed as if we walked at least ten miles before we spotted the distant glow of yard lights. It was certainly past midnight when we entered a village of a dozen darkened houses, each guarded by a barking dog. At the only intersection in town we turned toward the river and descended to an abandoned and rusting iron bridge that dead-ended in a wall of woods on the Wisconsin side. In the pocket of my swimsuit was a book of paper matches that had somehow remained dry. We gathered deadfalls and built a fire.

At some point, very early in the morning, while we huddled close to the fire, headlights danced in the trees and a truck crested the hill. The lights went off. A door closed. Mark walked down the bank and squatted next to the fire. He poked it with a stick.

"Been wondering where you guys were," he said.

"Is this Scott's Landing?"

"Not even close."

We had gone too far. Miles and miles too far. Mark had looked for us at every bridge and access site on fifty miles of the Brule.

"How did we miss it?"

"Easy," said Mark, in his best nonchalant drawl. "According to some guy at a gas station, Scott's Landing washed out in a flood in 1957 and the bridge was never replaced. Seems that out-of-towners are always getting lost looking for the damned thing."

Cast in Iron

MY COOKING SKILLS ARE MINIMAL, BUT WITH PERSISTENCE
I've learned to prepare a small repertoire of dishes. I can sauté
grouse and woodcock breasts, whip up a passable omelet,
hash-brown potatoes to that just-so texture and color (it requires more butter and patience than skill), and fry fresh
walleye fillets that will leave you shouting hoarsely for more.
I can prepare those things, moreover, on an open campfire.
But only on cast iron. Take away my old black skillet, and I
have to serve peanut-butter sandwiches and SpaghettiOs.

Like a lot of people, I used to think of cooking kits as
utensils. As such they were nuisances that had to be cleaned
periodically and lugged everywhere I went on camping trips.
I thought they had to be as light and compact as possible, with
aluminum or stainless-steel components that nested neatly inside one another until they made a package as tight and small
as the telescoping drinking cup I received for Christmas when
I joined the Cub Scouts. I took pride in seeing how little
space my cook kit required in my backpack.

The only problem was, I couldn't cook worth beans. I
blamed it on a privileged upbringing (Mom did most of the

cooking) and got into the habit of feasting in restaurants before and after my expeditions. In the bush I lived on trail mix,
jerky, and freeze-dried beef stew.

Then somewhere along the line—over a late breakfast, I
think, in an underheated apartment in Marquette, Michigan—
I discovered the ease and elegance of cooking with cast iron,
and my life was changed.

It's hard to mess up a meal in cast iron. Iron distributes
heat more slowly and evenly than stainless steel, aluminum,
or copper, and is therefore more forgiving than those tem-
pestuous, fast-heating materials. Iron seems most at home
over open fires, balanced nicely on three well-chosen stones,
but works equally well on a charcoal grill or propane stove.
Drop a slab of butter into a hot skillet and it sizzles in a satisfying way, sliding on its own liquid trail to the downhill
side, gathering in a golden, molten pool. No mad, manic
spattering—it sizzles serenely, like the difference between a
fire of split oak and one of pine kindling. Crack an egg on
the edge of the skillet, and the white spreads over the hot
butter without sticking to the pan, without burning at the
edges, without breaking at the yolk when a spatula is slipped
beneath for that critical flip.

Collectors prowl flea markets and auctions in search of
fine old Wagners and Griswolds, the Old Towns and Peter-
boroughs of skillets. But cast-iron cookware is not limited to
frying pans. Dutch ovens, kettles, griddles, even muffin pans
have been made of iron. One evening in the Canadian Rockies my wife demonstrated some of the versatility of cast iron
by baking a cake in a Dutch oven. She half-buried it in a bed
of coals, heaped more coals on the lid, and, after a duration
of time arrived at by intuition and arcane knowledge, with-
drew it from the coals and produced a superb pineapple
upside-down cake. I was deeply impressed.

Iron cookware is made pretty much the same way it was made one hundred years ago, in pretty much the same styles. The skillets are numbered, like fishhooks and nails, following a code of uniformity. My favorite is #6, measuring nine and three-eighths inches across—just right for fried potatoes for two, or hash browns, eggs, and bacon for one. I also like the fact that if properly seasoned with oil, cast-iron skillets require little more than a swipe with a paper towel to clean. If they get too grungy you can dip them in the fire or cook them in an oven to burn away the residue of past meals. Every few months you can wash them with soap and water, re-season them with hot cooking oil, and they're as good as new.

Admittedly iron skillets are heavy, take up precious space, are heavy, lack shine, are heavy, tend to get pitted after long use, and are heavy. Did I mention they're heavy? My #6 weighs more than my sleeping bag and spare paddle combined, weighs more than a week's supply of trail mix or a three-day ration of beef stew, weighs more than the collected short stories of Wallace Stegner (hardcover). I accept that. On portages I make an extra trip. Around camp I rest longer to make up for the additional effort and pass the time daydreaming about twelve-inch brook trout simmering in *sauce normande*.

Going Buggy

For reasons yet to be explained, biting insects have a special affection for people confined to canoes and kayaks. Regular harassment by black flies and mosquitoes—as well as deer flies, horse flies, sand flies, moose flies, midges, gnats, no-see-ums, and ticks—ensures that paddlers will always run out to buy any product that promises relief. I've got a shelf full of sprays and lotions, but so far have resisted dressing in Bug Baffler's DEET-impregnated clothing (about seventy-five dollars for hooded shirt and pants). I'm saving it for the last line of defense.

DEET—or diethyl toluamide—is the defensive weapon of choice in the war against stingers, biters, chewers, and suckers. Though it works better than any chemical formulated so far, I worry that full-body immersion in the stuff might have undesirable side effects. It bothers me, for instance, that my fingers go numb when I lather up with Deep Woods Off. When a buddy of mine slathered his legs, arms, neck, and face with a commercial repellent consisting of 100 percent DEET, he went into shock, vomited, passed out, underwent mild convulsions, and for several days suffered severe headaches and stomach cramps. Milder products like Tender's Natrapel put my mind at ease—especially when the kids need dosing—but, alas, they don't work as well.

The earliest insect repellents were probably smoky fires, mud baths, and regular spongings with bear grease. The nineteenth-century writer known as Nessmuk, author of numerous popular books on camp lore, recommended the following recipe (and dubious hints for personal hygiene): "3 oz. pine tar, 2 oz. castor oil, 1 oz. pennyroyal oil. Simmer all together over a slow fire, and bottle for use. . . . Rub it in thoroughly and liberally at first, and after you have established a good glaze, a little replenishing from day to day will be sufficient. And don't fool with soap and towels where insects are plenty. . . . Last summer I carried a cake of soap and a towel in my knapsack through the North Woods for a seven weeks' tour, and never used either a single time."

Other shotgun recipes from years past included such ingredients as black tar, petroleum jelly, citronella, cloves, camphor, lavender, oil of eucalyptus, oil of cedar, sassafras, creosote, carbolic acid, kerosene, melted sheep fat—in short, any heavily scented substance that could adhere to human skin without irritating it beyond endurance.

Mosquitoes, most of the time, are fairly easy to get along with. A light dose of a repellent does the job nicely. Besides, for me at least, their lazy whining conjures memories of past canoe trips, of fishing for bass at night with my father, of exploring brook-trout streams in cedar swamps. If you've forgotten your repellent you can avoid the heaviest concentrations of mosquitoes by camping on windy points and staying clear of the wet, shady places where they hang out. They're direct and single-minded and sluggish enough to be vulnerable to a well-timed slap. If you're inclined toward vengeance you can even clap them in midair, their hollow bodies smashing to a satisfying flatness in your palms.

Flies are less tolerable. Black flies of the genus *Simulium* are among the most dreaded of the biter-lappers, partly because they inhabit northern regions and are dependent on clean, cold, fast-running rivers—the same places many of us prefer to spend our time—but mostly because they hatch in such enormous numbers. Individually they're slow, clumsy fliers and have a tendency to crawl around on your skin for a few moments before dining, which makes them vulnerable. But when they're out in full force they simply overwhelm you. Not even head nets, strong repellents, and tight-fitting sleeves and cuffs can stop them from reaching your skin and gnawing. They're particularly fond of such tender areas as wrists, ankles, and the backs of ears. Their bite draws blood. And hurts. Stories of people driven insane and of moose sucked dry of blood are probably not exaggerated.

Deer flies hang around in the bushes along shore, then bombard paddlers as they pass. Here in the Midwest they're most active during the peak of summer, when our guards are down (mosquitoes and black flies have eased off by then) and we're likely to have replaced our bottles of repellent with bottles of suntan lotion. Not that it matters. Repellent seems only to irritate deer flies, inspiring them to more frenzied flight and more determined attacks. They don't swarm like black flies, preferring to attack blindly, in kamikaze rushes, diving into your hair or onto your shoulder, inflicting a bite as sharp as a needle jab, then escaping.

One summer afternoon a few years ago Craig Date and I were harassed to distraction by deer flies on Michigan's Manistique River. It was a beautiful day but the flies were so vicious we had no chance to enjoy it. They circled us in manic orbits, diving in one after another to attack unprotected flesh. Our efforts to outrace them were futile, and we were reduced to paddling most of the river one-handed, using our free hands to wave the flies off as best we could. At the end of the trip I ran for the ten-speed bike we had stashed in the bushes as a shuttle vehicle, thinking I could get some relief on the open road. Craig took cover beneath the overturned canoe to wait until I returned with the truck.

A rabble of a dozen or so flies stayed with me while I pedaled down a gravel road to its junction with the highway. Once on the pavement I was confident I would leave them behind. I came to a long downhill stretch, shifted to high gear, leaned low over the handlebars, and pedaled. I pedaled as hard as I could. I'm sure I reached twenty-five miles per hour. Yet the deer flies had no trouble keeping pace. They flew along at what appeared to be a leisurely pace. For a few crazy minutes I thought they were toying with me.

They had dined on my blood all afternoon, leaving welts on my scalp and neck, and now, when I thought I had reached a hill long enough and steep enough to outdistance the ghouls and get a few minutes of relief, I couldn't do it. I couldn't go fast enough to escape them. I was beaten. They weren't just keeping up, they were circling me.

Putting a Lid on It

EXCEPT DURING HUNTING SEASON, WHEN THE STATE mandates a cap of orange, I'm not much of a hat guy, usually preferring to keep my top open to the heavens with the hope that I won't miss something important. Still, I recognize the wisdom in occasionally putting a lid on the old dome. It's sometimes a good idea, for instance, to reduce the 60 percent of your body heat that leaks from the top of your head. There are times, too, when you want to stay dry in the rain, keep mosquitoes off your bald spot, and protect yourself beneath a mobile source of shade when an intense sun is raining showers of ultraviolet B. Hats can also make a powerful fashion statement. On the waters where I spend most of my time it has become de rigueur among young canoeists and fishermen to wear a baseball cap backwards, which seems a pretty good way to avoid sunburn on the nape of the neck but is neglectful of the nose and cheeks. A more sensible choice—and a fashion statement of its own—might be a full-brimmed hat like the Tilly Endurable.

Now *that's* a hat. Ten-ounce cotton duck. Preshrunk, water repellent. Has a rugged woodsy look yet is advertised in *The New Yorker*. Doesn't lose its shape with use. Is tough enough to swat out a brushfire. The manufacturer claims it is "the best, most practical outdoor hat in the world," which he obviously believes since the hat is guaranteed for the life of the wearer. Anyone who owns a Tilly tends to become attached to it.

People have always had a special attachment to hats, perhaps because they play such an important role in the images we create for ourselves. Hats advertise character, announcing to the world that we're adventurers, rebels, conservatives, or jocks. They're also a good way to hide bad hair and add a couple inches of height. Often they're one of the initial things you notice about a person, contributing much to that all-important first impression.

A passion for hats was in part responsible for inspiring Europeans to climb into bark canoes and explore the Old Northwest during the seventeenth and eighteenth centuries. The French Canadian voyageurs of that era journeyed into the wilderness to the west and north of the Great Lakes in search of beaver pelts, which they took in trade for rifles, axes, traps, whiskey, and other goods. In pursuit of that lucrative trade, thirty-five-foot bark canoes and their crews of eight or ten voyageurs would set out from Montreal in May every year. After six weeks and thirty-six portages they would reach Grand Portage or Fort William at the western end of Lake Superior, where they would unload their cargo of trade goods and load up with three or four tons of pelts worth a small fortune. If luck and weather were with them, they made it back to Montreal by October, before ice clogged the rivers. The furs continued by sailing vessel down the St. Lawrence and across the Atlantic to feed a seemingly insatiable appetite for beaver hats of one sort or another, which for a century and a half were all the rage in the salons and ballrooms of

England, France, and Germany. In the first decades of the nineteenth century, styles like the Wellington, D'Orsay, Paris Beau, and Regent were so popular they were worn both indoors and out. No gentleman would dream of being seen without one.

Judging from paintings of the era, the voyageurs themselves were fond of a variety of hats, ranging from bandannas to floppy cowboylike styles to a sort of fez adorned with a bright sash and feather. The main idea then as now was to keep water and insects off the head and provide warmth in the cold, but you can tell there was a lot of fashion consciousness going around even in the wilderness.

In my office is a shelf stacked with hats I've acquired during my travels. Many are baseball caps adorned with company logos and slogans, some so vapid that I wouldn't be caught dead in them. One or two have made their way to my fishing closet, where I grab them on the way to the river. My favorite, a gift from a local conservation group, announces that I'm an Au Sable River Watcher. I wear it much of the time while fishing, especially on bright afternoons and at night, when mosquitoes would otherwise attack my skull. It's become a regular part of my attire, but I'm always a bit relieved to take it off when I get back to the truck.

I suppose I'm waiting to find the perfect hat. The Tilly comes close, but it doesn't get around some basic shortcomings. I like to feel the wind in my hair and the hot breath of the sun on my scalp, and I don't mind a little rain. In cold weather or a downpour or when the black flies are being particularly evil or if I need to cut down on the glare to see while fishing, I'll relent and put on whatever's at hand. If it's a baseball cap and I'm in the mood, I might even wear it backwards.

Getting Out

AMONG THE FEW THINGS I KNOW FOR CERTAIN ARE
that wet wool has less insulating value than the experts claim,
that Kraft Macaroni & Cheese is one food—perhaps the only
food—that tastes worse cooked over an open fire, and that
forty million bumper stickers can't be wrong when they say
a bad day of fishing is better than a good day of working.

The wisdom of those bumper stickers was proved true
recently during a visit to a friend's cabin near the end of the
Keweenaw Peninsula, where Upper Michigan pokes its finger
into the belly of Lake Superior. It's a place so far removed
from Detroit—both in miles and spirit—that they might as
well be on separate continents. Though I live about halfway
between those two extremes, my sympathies definitely lean
north.

I drove there on a day that had begun bright and prom-
ising, but once I got past L'Anse the sky clouded over and a
light drizzle began to fall. By the time I reached Jim's cabin
near the northern point of the Keweenaw, the rain was coming down in a steady downpour. It didn't stop for two days.

Jim, Ron, and I hadn't seen each other in nearly a year,

so there was plenty to talk about. We built a fire in the stove, threw together a memorable meal, and caught up on things. The weather was dismal—cold wind and relentless rain, the kind that turns gravel roads to oatmeal and two-tracks to twin rivers. It was a weekend better suited to cribbage and thick novels than to outdoor pursuits.

We were patient that first day, but after twenty-four hours Ron and I couldn't sit around any longer. Jim is a conservation officer and a native of the Upper Peninsula—a Yooper—who's been stomping around in the Keweenaw and the rest of the UP all of his life. He wasn't keen on going out in the rain, but he told us about a good lake nearby and plotted a course for us on a topo map. Ron and I put on our rain gear and went outside to load Jim's canoe on the truck.

I was a little disappointed in the canoe. It was short and squat, made of dented aluminum, and painted army green. Strips of foam had been glued to the inside of the gunwales for flotation, and an outboard-motor mount was bolted to the stern. One seat was broken and had to be propped up with a chunk of two-by-four. But we were in no position to be choosy. We threw it on and tied it down. Jim waved from the door as we spun up the driveway.

The lake sat at the end of seven miles of overflowing two-tracks, in a valley between hills of hardwoods and pines. It wasn't pretty: one hundred acres of whitecaps and weed beds with drowned cedars ringing the shores. Gray clouds scudded past overhead, shredded by powerful winds off Lake Superior. A couple of miles away the shore of Superior was being battered by enormous waves. The ground shuddered faintly. Even in the woods you could sense the immensity out there.

The little lake was supposed to be full of big northern pike so vicious they would charge our lures like Dobermans. A friend from Marquette had said he caught dozens there the previous year, many in the six-to-eight-pound class. We couldn't wait. We had been working too hard of late and needed this as therapy. It took maybe five minutes to run the canoe to the shore, toss in our gear, and push off.

The canoe caught the wind and sailed. Even with rain slanting into our faces and wind yanking the rain hoods from our heads, our guts clenched in anticipation. We cast our lures with the conviction that discomfort is sometimes rewarded. We cast into shallow water and we cast into deep water, over weed beds and over rocks and into godawful tangles of drift-wood and stumps. We tried deerhair poppers and outra-geously gaudy streamers and Daredevls and Mepps Spinners and Rapalas and Bombers and a muskie lure twice as big as most of the brook trout living in Upper Michigan. But we caught nothing. Not a thing. In three hours and maybe three-hundred casts we did not have a single strike.

At some point we realized that our efforts were futile. We had theories: low-pressure system. Wind from the east, fish bite the least. Too much rain, and the fish get sated with drowned creatures.

We also realized, to our surprise, that we liked the little canoe. It was fat and ugly, it was broken, it may have been designed by a military engineer whose previous experience had been with portable pontoon bridges, yet it was responsive and deft and stable in the waves. In spite of our paddles—inexpensive wooden beavertails, the varnish long vaporized, one with a blade split lengthwise and so warped that it looked like a lobster claw on a stick—we made good progress against the wind. We found ourselves laughing and singing as we paddled. We wished the lake were bigger and linked by chan-nels with others we could explore. On this bad day of fishing there was no place we would have rather been.

At noon we pulled up on the shore of an island and found

one of the world's finest pine-sheltered campsites. The ground was spongy with a couple of centuries' worth of needle drop, and you could look beyond the trees in three directions and see water. We sat on old, mossy stumps with the rain falling around us and ate a lunch of French bread, cheese, liverwurst, and crisp McIntoshes. Ragged flocks of ducks rocketed over the lake, then wheeled and set their wings and came in hard against the wind and the whitecaps. Ron and I looked at each other and grinned. Jim was back in the cabin alone, probably reading a novel by the stove, warm and dry.

We couldn't wait to rub it in.

A Good Night's Sleep

SLEEP KNITS UP THE RAVELED SLEEVE OF CARE, AND since I sleep as badly as that poor wretch Macbeth, I need to take every advantage I can get. When I'm camping I want a real pillow and an ample sleeping pad spread on a spot that is flat and free of rocks and roots. And I want the best sleeping bag possible, which, as everyone knows, means a bag lined with several ounces of the finest, fluffiest goose down you can sink a tired body into.

The problem is, I don't own a down sleeping bag—never have—so what I know about the subject comes mostly from secondhand sources. I've borrowed down bags a few times, and several of my friends own them and swear by them, but I won't be able to buy one myself until I overcome a couple of problems. First, I can't forget the two days and nights a buddy and I passed camping in the rain in Glacier National Park and the fact that later, after we spent a night in a Missoula motel with our gear draped over the furniture and the furnace turned up as high as it would go, my cheap bag of synthetic fill was as dry as week-old wedding cake and John's expensive down bag was a wadded wet mess that looked as if it had just been yanked from the spin cycle of a washing machine. Also, I can't afford to spend a week's wages for a bag of feathers. I have kids to feed and a new canoe to pay for. Tell the boss I need a raise.

But if the day comes when I *can* afford it, I won't hesitate to hand over the money, because it's well-known that sleeping on down is the best way on earth to get a good night's sleep. Feathers and bedding have been wedded for centuries, since long before Ben Franklin's feather bed and the eiderdown sleeping bags popular at the turn of the twentieth century and the latest goose-down bags with their shells of waterproof DryLoft (which is nearly as waterproof as Gore-Tex and 66 percent more breathable). Feathers make excellent places to sleep, for several reasons. Down weighs considerably less than even the best synthetic fillers, is incredibly efficient at keeping birds and humans warm, compresses to a small package, and has a very long loft life, which means it stays fluffy for ages. Down also happens to be as light and soft as angel's breath, as gentle as a spring creek, and as soothing as children's laughter. It seems to be the very stuff sweet dreams are made of.

SLEEPING BAGS WORK on simple principles. They trap body heat by creating a layer of dead air space, and nothing makes more dead air space than the downy feathers that lie against the skin of geese and ducks. The stuff is remarkably efficient at keeping waterfowl toasty warm, even in Arctic seas. When a brooding goose lines its nest with down plucked from its own breast, it creates a bed warm enough to keep a featherless gosling alive even in nasty April weather. But it is not just its insulating value that makes down so ideal. Sleeping bags go through hell. They're stuffed into the smallest bundles possible for storage and transport, then are spread on the ground and squashed flat by sweating two-hundred-pound humans. Packed tight, even the best insulators lose their value; without trapped air they provide no protection from the cold. But give a down bag a brisk shake and it fluffs up again and immediately goes to work trapping air. It's darned-near perfect for the job.

The quality of the down in a sleeping bag is rated by its fluffiness, or loft. Cheap bags are usually labeled "down filled," and can contain up to 20 percent feathers—complete with stems—which makes them less compactible and less efficient, and reduces loft. Bags labeled "100 percent down" are exactly that—all down, no feathers. Their loft is rated by "fill power," an industry standard measured in cubic inches of loft per ounce of down. A 550-fill rating means that an ounce of the down used will loft to a volume of 550 cubic inches. The best down is 700-fill and is usually reserved for bags designed for subzero temperatures.

Some of the new synthetic fillers manage to come close to the efficiency of down, and nearly match it in weight and compressibility. But they aren't the same. They can be light and fluffy and warm, but they still feel synthetic. It's like the difference between a hotel pillow and your good down pillow back home. You just can't reproduce the luxurious feel of the real thing.

If you can combine a good sleeping bag with a good sleeping pad—I'm partial to Therm-A-Rest, the original self-inflating mattress, and especially to the luxury edition, with its nonslip Staytek fabric—you're guaranteed a good night's sleep. Dylan, the salesclerk at our local outfitting shop, insists that if I "invest" (his word) $450 for the new North Face Foxfire/DL, my sleep will be so sound that every morning I'll be several minutes younger than I was when I went to sleep. He promises that four hours in the 700-fill Foxfire is more restful than eight hours in any other bag. I'll sleep like a mountain, he says. My sleep will be so peaceful that I'll send harmonic waves of goodness to troubled regions all over the globe. It'll feel as if I'm riding a feather bed downstream on a quiet river at night, the quarter moon cresting a ridge of cottonwoods, night creatures lined up on the banks cooing lullabies.

"What if it rains?" I ask.

"Dude," Dylan says, horror on his face, "never, never get the bag wet. I'm totally serious. Water turns it into goose mulch. And it takes like an eternity to dry out."

Heading North

THOSE OF US WHO AUTOMATICALLY TURN NORTH WHEN we need replenishment find Canada both comforting and distressing. Comforting because no matter how crowded our home waters become, thousands of lakes and rivers in Canada remain undisturbed. Distressing because we know that those lakes and rivers will not be undisturbed forever. We are too many, and no place is safe from encroachment.

As often happens, we suffer from conflicting urges. We need a portion of the world to remain unexplored, yet we are driven by an innate urge to explore. Those who care try to leave as little evidence of their passing as possible. That's the great advantage of canoeing and kayaking, and the justification for the low-impact camping ethic: It makes it possible to journey to the great Canadian outback and not destroy it.

When you've traveled by canoe in Canada, you can never forget the qualities of the country. It is vast and unspoiled, with water so clear you can count pebbles on the bottom forty feet down, and air so crisp it's like snorting shots of pure oxygen. I can't recall a single outing that has not been highlighted by encounters with bears, moose, caribou, coyotes, and wolves. I think back to August mornings on a high mountain lake in the Canadian Rockies where I discovered that rainbow trout would surge forward and engulf a grasshopper imitation if I splatted it next to shore and made it pop and swim like a living thing. I remember fat native cutthroat trout in Alberta rivers, where they flowed east from the foothills of the Rockies and wound in great sweeping meanders across the plains. I remember Ontario lakes so full of northern pike that they slashed at a lure even after it was clamped in another pike's jaws and sometimes forced me to battle two fish at once. I remember smallmouth bass in New Brunswick rivers and brook trout from the ponds that dot the Newfoundland tundra like seeds broadcast by a titan's hand. I remember standing on a rock escarpment in Quebec looking across a hundred square miles of country free of roads and houses, and growing giddy with the possibility that I had every bit of it to myself.

Thank God Canada is big. It sprawls across more than 3.8 million square miles, and most of it is absolutely crammed with water. The Northwest Territories alone cover 1.25 million square miles, an area larger than all the states east of the Mississippi combined and home to more than 9 percent of the freshwater on the surface of the earth. Most of the Yukon and Northwest Territories and the northern portions of British Columbia, Alberta, Saskatchewan, Manitoba, Ontario, Quebec, and Labrador contain so much water that a resolute adventurer with a canoe, enough food, and deep reserves of determination could paddle many hundreds of miles of rivers and linked lakes without portaging more than a few miles at a time. If you had the resources and the patience, you could go weeks without setting foot on land.

But not every journey to Canada's wilderness has to be a major expedition. When time is short—and it almost always is—I opt for a budget trip. I drive most of the night, pull into a quiet spot beside a river for a two-hour nap in the truck, and have a breakfast of apples and sandwiches from the cooler. By midmorning I can be someplace remote.

Many of my most enjoyable trips over the years have been in Ontario north of Sault Ste. Marie, within two hundred miles of home. For years my usual tactic was to head west or northeast out of the Soo, then take the north fork at every intersection until the pavement gave way to gravel and the telephone lines disappeared, then after fifty or one hundred miles stop at a lake and launch my canoe. You can reach fine country and outstanding fishing this way. You paddle the length of the lake to the mouth of a tributary river and follow it upstream until you reach the first rapids. Portage the rapids, paddle two or three miles to where the river widens into a small lake, cross to the falls on the far shore and find the hidden portage trail leading to the next lake. The best campsite is beneath the pines on the island in the middle of that lake.

I'm remembering a particular island, of course, on a particular lake. It's a place I visited for the first time more than twenty years ago and immediately began thinking of as my own. That first morning, early, while the sun beamed pink on the pines and the water was so calm it looked as if you could skate across it, I rolled out of my tent, pulled on my jeans and a pair of sneakers, grabbed my spinning rod, and walked fifteen feet to the water's edge. I cast a red-and-white Daredevl, the lure of choice across much of Canada, and watched it soar far out into the lake and slice the surface of the water. It was an act of faith. I had never fished the lake and did not know if it was home to pike or bass or trout or to any fish at all.

As I retrieved the lure I listened to the first rustle of the breeze in the trees and knew that this far upstream from the main lake I would not hear automobiles or outboards. Later in the morning a floatplane would pass high overhead, bound for some lodge or tent camp to the north. It would be the only engine I heard during my stay on the island. Someone else had once camped there—they had left a ring of stones around charred fragments of wood—but it was hard to tell if the camp was a year old or a decade old. There were no other signs of humans. I could have been in northern Labrador or the interior of British Columbia. I could have been an explorer laying claim to a thousand square miles of wilderness.

On that first cast a five-pound northern pike slammed the lure. The fish turned out to be a little bigger than average for pike in that lake, but what they lacked in size they made up for in abundance. And they seemed always to be in the mood for a fight.

CANADA HAS AN appeal much greater than the quality of its fishing and the beauty of its water and land. Whether you're on a lake in the Laurentian-shield country above Lake Superior, in the taiga of northern Quebec, or in the old-growth forests of British Columbia, the great attraction of the place— I'm tempted to say the magic of it—comes from an exciting, virtually palpable sense of possibility. Even in the cities and the relatively civilized portions of the nation, you can sense the presence of all that vast unspoiled land to the north. It's in the air as surely as the scent of pines and the sound of running water.

Most of the remaining wild country in North America is in Canada. It's the last priceless reserve, the place against which we measure all other places, and a reminder of how much has been lost from the world.

Great Blades

W HEN THE CALL GOES OUT AROUND A CAMPFIRE OR A busted canoe or a tangle of hopelessly knotted ropes— "Who's got a knife?"—your hand goes to your pocket and the knife is there, ready for use: the right tool for the job, an emblem of the pride you take in owning a few good things. With a pocketknife the pride goes back decades, to the first one you owned when you were a kid. Mine, a gift from my father when I was ten, was a folding black jackknife with a can opener, a leather punch, and a single blade worn thin from whetting and darkened to the color of old nickels. It had been Dad's first knife, and passing it to me was weighted with significance. It was a rite of passage, an initiation, and a handing off of family torch all in one. With it came responsibilities. It was not a toy. It was not to be thrown or handled carelessly. It was never to be passed blade first to another person. It was a man's solemn accoutrement, beautiful in its utility, always sharp and clean, always ready in case of emergency.

Such serious business lingers. All these years later it still feels good to carry a knife—a folding one for my pocket when traveling in polite society, a sheath knife on my hip when hunting or camping in wild country. Though my father's old knife is long lost, left beside a brook-trout stream fifteen years ago and never recovered, a knife snug in the pocket of my jeans still gives a comforting sense of readiness and responsibility. I've given each of my sons his own pocketknife and tried to impart the respect I learned at their ages. It's not a toy, I emphasize, and their eyes grow bright with understanding. They're glad. By the age of ten or twelve, most boys are ready to start giving up toys for tools.

Of course the knife has to be a good one, made of fine steel and built with care. It must be strong, it must hold an edge, and it must fit comfortably in its owner's hand. The pinnacle of knife making has always been reached not in factories but in small workshops run by solitary craftsmen. Such craftsmen can be divided into two groups. One uses a technique known as stock removal, in which they begin with a piece of steel (usually alloy steel composed of various elements) and cut and grind away everything that doesn't look like a knife. The other favors a technique known as blade-smithing (or forging), an ancient method using fire and a hammer to shape a piece of high-carbon steel into a knife.

Knife makers differentiate between collectible knives— works of art suitable for display in museums and costing thousands of dollars—and "using" knives. Our relationship with knives is so intimate that for thousands of years craftsmen have gone to great trouble to make even their everyday blades attractive. And though you must pay a lot of money for the best custom knives, even the factory-built models for sale at the local hardware are fine tools. Some of those moderately priced production knives are so precisely tooled and so satisfying to the eye and hand that they give pleasure every time they're used.

But there's a downside. Where pleasure is great, so is pain, and it is intensely painful to lose a good blade. Years ago, while paddling across a lake in Ontario, I pulled my Gerber hunting knife from its sheath to pry a leech from my leg. When I flicked it over the side of the canoe the leech went flying, but so did the knife. I can still see the flash of polished steel as it fluttered into the depths and disappeared.

And I can still see that single-bladed jackknife my dad gave me, sticking from a cedar log beside a pool on Jackson Creek. I had knelt beside the pool to gut a pair of ten-inch brook trout, then wiped the blade on moss and stuck it in the log. I washed the brookies in the creek and arranged them on a bed of sweet fern in my creel. The scent of the ferns made me think of other trout on other streams and perhaps sent me into a culinary reverie, imagining how I would split the trout lengthwise, roll them in flour, fry them in oil, and serve them with morels and asparagus and very cold beer. I slung the creel over my shoulder, gathered my rod, and struck out through the cedars for the road.

Though I went back a half dozen times, I never found the pool again. The swamp is big and the creek has several branches. After a few tries I gave up hope of finding the knife and came to appreciate the idea of it growing rusty in the log beside the secret pool.

Places like that are sometimes better when we never return. We stumble upon them in our usual blind way and enjoy a few special moments, then wander off on another path. In the process, in a kind of barter with the world, we take something precious away and leave something precious behind.

Seems like a fair swap.

Real Food

LATELY MY TEENAGE SON, AARON, HAS BEEN TASTE-testing meals of dehydrated backpacking food, but I'm not sure he makes a valid subject for such experiments. He's at that stage where he'll eat just about anything and is growing so fast that at night you can hear his bones groaning and creaking, like steel girders expanding in the sun. In the middle of a recent dinner, bent in concentration over his plate, he looked up with a worried expression and said, "Even while I'm *eating* I'm getting hungry." His opinion of what's currently available in dried and freeze-dried foods? "Pretty good," he says. "Kind of chewy."

I've sampled the dishes myself and am especially impressed with "Black Bean Tamale Pie" from Backpacker's Pantry, Mountain House's "Chicken à la King," and both the taco-pita filling and the pizza (really) available from Adventure Foods. Almost as good are AlpineAire's "Santa Fe Black Beans and Rice," Backpacker's Pantry's "Chili Cheese Nachos," Natural High's "Zucchini Lasagna," and Wee-Pak's "Sour-Cream Turkey." Without exception all the dehydrated meals we've been testing improved after they were soaked in water twice as long as the recommended ten minutes, and most were even better when heated up as leftovers the next day. The Mexican dishes are especially good, but they're so mild that anyone who likes their food to bite back will want to season generously with jalapeños, chili pepper, or hot sauce. All in all, prepared trail foods are compact, flavorful, and convenient—the outdoor equivalent of microwave dinners.

I admit to having some mixed feelings. One of the reasons I prefer canoes over backpacks is that canoes make it possible to carry real potatoes instead of instant ones. On the other hand, I don't want to spend hours preparing a dinner when I can be exploring, fishing, or loafing instead. Is there a compromise between fast food and slow food in the outdoors? Maybe. By serving the best of the new dehydrated meals with a mixture of fresh foods and liberal amounts of garlic, herbs, and spices, you can devise cuisine that's both satisfying and convenient. My entire family was pleased with a recent dinner that included Mountain House's stroganoff over pasta. And I prepared it indoors, on the kitchen stove—conditions that would have made the dehydrated beef stew we ate while camping ten years ago unpalatable. That standard stew, incidentally, is still available. When I served it to my family not long ago, Nick took one look at it heaped on his plate, crinkled up his nose, made an ugly noise, and said, "No way am I eating *that*."

You have to wonder how he'd react to pemmican and bannock. Those staples of old-time (and some contemporary) wilderness trippers have been praised loud and long for their nutritive value, their convenience, and even, now and then, their tastiness. During expeditions in the Far North, caloric requirements can be twice what they are in the normal world, putting a premium on fat. Bannock—fried pan bread—is still popular in some circles, but it must be made the traditional way: with white flour, baking soda, and salt mixed with a small amount of river water and kneaded into dough with copious amounts of melted bear lard ("The secret is to use more lard than you can possibly imagine—and then some," writes a correspondent). The dough can be flavored with raisins, cranberries, or blueberries. Punch it down and spread it about an inch thick in a cast-iron skillet smoking with hot lard, then prop it in front of a roaring fire and bake it to a golden brown, flip once, and serve. Hard-core woodsmen eat it slathered with lard and salt, but you might prefer jam.

The voyageurs of the Great Lakes ate a standard gruel consisting of peas, corn mush, and water mixed with pork fat. When they headed inland, north and west of Lake Superior, they relied on pemmican made of dried and shredded bison meat mixed with lard rendered from buffalo fat and spiced with dried berries. The stuff could be eaten raw or cooked and if sealed in buffalo-hide sacks would last for months— even years—without refrigeration. Not incidentally, it was packed with calories. While traveling by canoe, the *hivernants,* voyageurs who wintered in the interior beyond Superior, got by on two meals a day of boiled pemmican. Sometimes they varied the menu by mixing pemmican with flour and water, adding a little maple syrup for flavoring, and making a soup called "rubbaboo."

Some modern expeditions, like Will Steger's 1986 dogsled run to the North Pole, and his 3,700-mile crossing of Antarctica by dogsled in 1989, rely on the high-caloric punch provided by old-style pemmican. Members of both Steger expeditions needed up to seven thousand calories a day each to remain fueled and warm—about twice what you need for a normal day's work in the civilized world. Most of those calories came from an evening meal consisting of pemmican of dried beef and lard cut up and thawed on a stove and served over noodles.

Caloric content was also the point of the main daily meal eaten during an ill-fated canoe expedition across the Barren Grounds of subarctic Canada in 1955. *A Death on the Barrens,* an account of the expedition written by survivor George James Grinnell, is a fascinating study of humans under duress. Until they ran out of provisions, the six members of the expedition subsisted on "glop" they made by mixing two boxes of macaroni, two cans of tomato paste, two packages of dehydrated soup, and two cans of "Spork" or "Spam" into a gallon or two of boiling river water. The greasy canned meats, cut into bite-size chunks, were the prizes in the broth, and each member of the expedition tried to devise ways to scoop more of them into his bowl.

Even those of us who engage in less ambitious expeditions become inordinately concerned with food when we spend all day outside. I'm always astonished at the volume of walleye and northern pike a party of paddlers can eat in the Ontario bush. In lakes and rivers where it's possible to catch a fish every cast, it sometimes seems that there aren't possibly enough fish in the water to curb your hunger. Elaborate bartering determines who gets the extra piece of fish—or the two or three cherries in a can of fruit cocktail. A roll of Life Savers begins to seem like a real lifesaver. A Hershey bar becomes as precious as a gold bar. You know food is becoming serious business when during lunch the favorite topic of conversation is dinner. If at breakfast everyone squats beside the fire, watching the pancakes with wolfish intensity, it's time to start hoarding cookies.

Tastes vary, of course, and not everyone gets equally voracious. Hemingway's Nick Adams was sent into raptures by raw onion sandwiches and canned beans mixed with ketchup.

Thoreau, though he spent a good share of his austere life outdoors, was evidently not much interested in food. In *The Maine Woods* he mentions that in preparation for an ascent of Mt. Katadin he downed a breakfast of "raw pork, a wafer of hard bread, and a dipper of condensed cloud or water spout." Even his diet on longer outings was notably lacking in quantity and imagination. His list of provisions for a twelve-day expedition for himself and two companions includes: "Soft hardbread, twenty-eight pounds; pork, sixteen pounds; sugar, twelve pounds; one pound black tea or three pounds coffee; one box or a pint of salt; one quart Indian meal, to fry fish in; six lemons, good to correct the pork and warm water; perhaps two or three pounds of rice, for variety. You will probably get some berries, fish, etc. besides."

If your luck is like mine, you've probably learned long ago that you can never count on those "berries, fish, etc." And if you're the sort who gets tired of raw pork and soft hardbread, you'd be wise to bring along a supply of freeze-dried Santa Fe chicken and Louisiana red beans and rice. Also, throw in some new potatoes, a sack of apples, a couple of pounds of cheddar, a few packages of nuts and raisins, and (believe me, you won't regret it) a dozen of the richest, sweetest chocolate bars you can find.

In Praise of Duct Tape

I ADMIT I'VE DONE SOME FOOLISH THINGS. ONE OF THE most foolish in recent memory was paddling a fiberglass canoe over a low, rocky ledge-drop on the Ocqueoc River. I have to share credit for that bright maneuver with my paddling partner, Craig Date, who was in the bow seat, and who insisted we could make it over the drop without harm to the boat if we paddled hard to get up speed and leaped it, ski-jump style. The bow (and Craig) made it over in fine shape, but the stern crashed on a jumble of rocks at the bottom, splitting our lovely and unmarred Sawyer like a ripe peach. A crack opened in the hull beneath the stern seat, and the river poured in.

We dragged the canoe to shore and turned it over to inspect the damage. It wasn't pretty. Shattered fiberglass lay exposed in a rip two feet long. There was nothing to do but eat a sandwich while waiting for the hull to dry in the sun. Then we applied duct tape, covering the crack in long, overlapping strips, pressing it into place with the rounded back of a pocketknife to squeeze out the air bubbles. The patch held for the remainder of the trip. It held, in fact, for the remainder of the summer.

Duct tape—also sometimes called "furnace tape" or "silver tape" or (in the case of the space-shuttle *Columbia* astronauts) "gray tape," in part to ease the considerable confusion that arises when the uninitiated think you are saying "duck" tape—deserves to be included with paper clips and needlenose pliers on everyone's list of handy inventions. Its origins are obscured by legend and myth, but apparently the tape dates to World War II. The 3M Company invented adhesive tape in the 1920s, but duct tape as we know it was invented during the war to answer the military's need for a strong tape that could be used for temporary repairs on aircraft, Jeeps, and other equipment. It also had to be waterproof—in part to keep ammunition boxes dry—and able to be ripped by hand, for quick use. The Johnson & Johnson Company answered the call and came up with a tape that combined cloth mesh, a rubber adhesive, and a rubberized coating. During the postwar building boom, furnace and air-conditioning installers discovered that Johnson & Johnson's military tape did a great job of binding and sealing ductwork. Previously, furnace ducts were put together with tape made of thin asbestos and paper wrapped and glued in place, or with liquid asbestos and gauze, which could be shaped much the way a plaster cast is shaped around a fractured leg. Duct tape made the job faster, easier, and certainly healthier.

Modern duct tape is so convenient and inexpensive that we tend to be cavalier about its use, forgetting that in the old days emergency repairs of canoeing and camping equipment required a witch's knack for concoctions. Canoe trippers carried bulky repair kits that included strips of rubber, packages of zinc oxide, and cans of white lead. A punctured canvas canoe had to be patched with materials at hand, say a hunk of cotton shirt coated with spruce resin. A split in the hull could be temporarily sealed, but it required an adhesive plaster patch made from zinc oxide mixed with water, warmed over a fire, and ironed into place with a hot knife. A shattered paddle could be made serviceable only by splinting and laboriously binding it with many yards of fishing line. In a pinch you could patch a hole in a canoe with a mixture of one part bacon grease with ten parts spruce gum, warmed in hot water.

Duct tape made all such tactics obsolete. With a roll of tape and a little ingenuity, it's possible to repair even the most seriously damaged canoe. Or canoe paddle. Or fishing rod. Or ax handle, tent, sleeping bag, rain jacket, backpack, or hiking boot. The stuff sticks to anything. Carpenters patch their leather nail aprons with it. Roofers use it to bind knee-pads to their jeans. My fifteen-year-old skateboarding neighbor gets additional mileage from his tattered Nikes by mummifying them with it. Years ago I used it to keep the muffler attached to my old Buick Special, in spite of the tape's tendency to raise a smokey stink when heated. It also kept a brake-light cover in place and the cracked sideview mirror from falling out of its frame. The authors of *The Duct Tape Book* and dozens of Internet websites (a recent search of the World Wide Web pulled up 6,750 pages of references to duct tape) list thousands of uses, from the practical (nonslip strips in the bottom of a bathtub; labels on floppy disks) to the whimsical (attaching your pets to the ceiling to get them out of the way while you vacuum) to the bizarre (cricket traps around the perimeter of a basement).

Without duct tape I would have floundered years ago. On short trips I take along a dozen yards of it wrapped carefully around a stick; on longer trips I bring an entire roll. It's as essential to a successful expedition as a pocketknife and matches. My canoe and I might come home battered and bruised and held together with telltale strips of gray, but by God we'll be in one piece.

Moccasins

I T'S AN AXIOM IN THE MILITARY THAT A SOLDIER IS ONLY as good as his feet. Paddlers know this to be true, which is why we're fastidious about changing our socks every day and wearing shoes and boots appropriate for the occasion. In our boats we prefer neoprene booties or waterproof Birkenstocks, and on portages appreciate the ankle support and no-slip traction of hiking boots. The key word in all matters of the feet is "comfort."

But comfort shouldn't end at the end of the day. Whether you wear synthetic booties, stay loyal to your old Bean boots, or insist on stewing all day in wet canvas sneakers, you'll want to slip into something dry and warm at the end of a trip. For pure comfort while hunkering next to a campfire or making the long drive home, nothing beats a pair of moccasins.

Moccasins were probably the first footwear devised by humans and have needed little improvement through the ages. A pair found on the feet of a 5,300-year-old frozen corpse in the Austrian Alps are little changed from those available from catalogs today. Their virtues are obvious. A simple moccasin of animal hide is warm and supple, forms naturally to your foot's shape, and is durable enough to outlast half a dozen pairs of Nikes and Reeboks. They weigh almost nothing and can be rolled up and tucked away in a tiny space. They dry quickly over a campfire. They never go out of style.

As kids many of us were convinced a pair of moccasins would allow us to sneak through the woods as quietly as Ojibwas (a tribe named, incidentally, for the distinctive way they puckered the seams on their moccasins). Horace Kephart expressed a similar view in 1917, in *Camping and Woodcraft*: "After one's feet have become accustomed to this most rational of all covering they become almost like hands, feeling their way, and avoiding obstacles as though gifted with a special sense. They can bend freely. One can climb in moccasins as in nothing else. So long as they are dry, he can cross narrow logs like a cat, and pass in safety along treacherous slopes where thick-soled shoes might bring him swiftly to grief. Moccasined feet feel the dry sticks underneath, and glide softly over the telltales without cracking them."

Kephart and most other campcraft authors recommend the properly tanned hide of a moose as the best material for moccasins, followed in order by caribou and elk. Most authorities agree that deerhide is too thin for good moccasins, although that soft and pliable skin makes a good sock to wear inside sturdier moccasins or to slip on for sleeping and lounging.

Commercially made moccasins are available in many outfitting shops and catalogs. L. L. Bean, for example, offers "Trapper Mocs" made of moosehide, a deluxe model equipped with ribbed PVC outer soles and fleece lining, for about half the price of a pair of Birkenstocks.

But if you have your heart set on traditional moccasins custom fitted to your feet, you'll probably have to make them yourself. The classic how-to book of life in the Canadian north, *Cache Lake Country* by John Rowlands, offers tips and patterns for making moccasins during long winter evenings when you have time on your hands. "Once you get on to the trick," the author promises, "it's not much of a job." Rowlands preferred a high-top version that wraps around the ankles and could be lined with an inner sock of doeskin for winter use. "Take your time, and don't rush the stitching," he writes. "Once you get the hang of puckering the toe and sewing in the vamp, the rest is easy."

When I was twelve years old and certain that I would spend my life alone in the Canadian wilderness, I was determined to master the art of puckering toes and sewing vamps. My first pair of moccasins came in kit form, just the thing for a kid setting out on the path of self-reliance. The kit was on display in the camping section of the local hardware store. I coveted it for months, until it had wormed its way into the life of my imagination. At night I would lie awake in the darkness and imagine myself stalking soundlessly through the woods, sneaking up on whitetails and cottontails, following my friends a crafty fifty feet behind. When I became lost and was forced to build a lean-to shelter, build a fire with flint and steel, and survive for months on game I snared and fish I speared, the moccasins would be a source of dependable comfort. I would dry them over the fire in the evenings and wear them to bed at night so I would be ready at any moment to leap to my feet, grab my spear, and defend myself.

I received the kit as a gift that Christmas. It consisted of two flat hunks of leather for soles, a pair of tonguelike vamps, two narrow strips for sides, a coil of lacing, and a mimeographed sheet of instructions. I spent day after day in my room sewing—pulling the coarse laces through prepunched holes in the leather, drawing on them until the pieces drew tight and the leather puckered. When, finally, I had finished the moccasins I put them on my bare feet and tried to walk. I couldn't. They were hard as plywood and cut into my toes and ankles with every step. I soaked the leather in the oil I used on my baseball glove and kneaded it for hours; I limped in agony up and down the driveway trying to break in the moccasins the way you might try to break the spirit of an iron-headed horse; I walked with them into the lake and allowed them to dry in place on my feet. Nothing helped. They remained as stiff as wooden clogs. I tried stalking through the woods anyway and was so loud and clumsy every animal for miles around fled in panic. Finally I threw them into the back of my closet and never wore them again. It took weeks for the blisters to heal.

So choose your leather carefully. Old-timers insist that the best moccasins are made from leather tanned the traditional way—with animal brains and plenty of kneading and stretching. Details like cutting and sewing get easier with practice. Armed with a sharp knife, a stout sewing needle, and unlimited free evenings, you'll eventually get the hang of it. You'll know when the job is done right. You'll slip that soft leather over your feet and glide through the woods as silently as an owl. You'll dance across wildflowers without crushing them. You'll run with the caribou and stalk with the lynx and handle every emergency with courage, strength, and flawless judgment. You'll be as graceful and light as sunbeams. You'll be a woodsman at last.

A River by Any Name

WHO CHRISTENS RIVERS? BY WHAT AUTHORITY DO they bless or curse harmless moving water?

My interest in such questions goes back years, to a time when I lived near a lively river named the Dead. Local historians claimed it was a name given in reference to a Chippewa burial ground located on its banks, but I suspected that such a fine trout river must have been named by an angler hoping to disguise its virtues. Had he been the protective father of a beautiful daughter he might have used the same impulse to dress her in dungarees and a baseball hat and call her Ralph.

But I'm afraid most rivers are named for less imaginative reasons. Here in Michigan we're stuck with five rivers named the Black. Colors have always been a popular and shamefully unchallenging source of river names. When you consider all the melodious and charming possibilities, mundane monikers such as the Black, the White, the Red, the Yellow, and the Green become inexcusable.

Scan an atlas, and you can get a pretty good idea of the state of imaginative resource in North America. It's heartening to note that there are plenty of rivers with the kinds of lovely and lyrical titles you sometimes find on watercolor paintings, poems, or old-time folk songs—names like the Sweetwater and Firehole in Wyoming, the Swift Diamond in New Hampshire, the Neversink in New York, the Vermillion in Illinois (a color name with panache), the White Top Laurel in Virginia, the Looking Glass in Michigan, and the Marais des Cygnes ("Marsh of Swans") in Missouri. Others, like the Hangman in Washington and the Bear-in-the-Lodge in South Dakota, conjure events from a colorful past.

On the other hand, some streams, like the Misery in Michigan, the Stinking Water and the Dismal in Nebraska, and the Skunk in Iowa are burdened with names that seem to have been conferred by people bent down by hard luck and disappointment.

Naming rivers after animals has always been popular, probably among the same folks who so heavily favor colors. There are entire herds of Buffalos, Rabbits, Bulls, Bears, and Turtles; whole flocks of Turkeys, Owls, Crows, and Swans. Oklahoma has a Wildhorse, Montana a Beaverhead, South Dakota a Dog Ear, and Texas a Prairie Dog Town Fork of the Red.

Names derived from Native American sources are a fine thing when the results are as melodious as the Kickapoo in Wisconsin and the Klickitat and Skookumchuck in Washington. Others, like the Ichawaynochaway in Georgia, the Conococheague in Pennsylvania, and the Ompompanoosuc in Vermont can be perennial sources of confusion for tourists and cartographers.

Most of the rivers I'm personally acquainted with—the Jordan, the Rapid, and the Crystal, for instance—have pleasant, if uninspired, names. The Au Sable has an elegant, continental air to it, though it loses something in translation

("River of Sand"). Others, like the Boardman and Platte, are less enchanting. Names of people should never be tacked on rivers. They should be left in telephone books or hung on a shingle: Platte and Boardman, Attorneys at Law.

I once set out to discover the source of one of America's loveliest and best-remembered river names, the Two Hearted. Located in Michigan's Upper Peninsula, that river attained superstar status soon after the publication of perhaps the most famous short story in twentieth-century America, Ernest Hemingway's "Big Two-Hearted River." Almost everyone knows by now that the river in "Big Two-Hearted River" is not the Two Hearted, but the Fox, which is located some forty miles south of it. The reason for the deception should be obvious. As Hemingway explained once in a letter to his father, he chose the Two Hearted because "it's poetry."

Indeed. I agree with my whole heart. With two hearts, if I had them. In certain moods I once imagined the river named by a Chippewa warrior whose breast was cleaved by love. Or, perhaps, named by someone who stood on the dunes at the mouth of the river, witnessed the expansive horizons of Lake Superior, and was overcome with the need for twice the heart to perceive and hold so much beauty.

It was a pilgrimage of sorts that took me to the Two Hearted. I came to canoe it, to camp along it, to fish for brook trout in the quick, shallow rapids in the upper reaches. I came to burrow to the heart of the river and comprehend firsthand the impulse behind its name.

Near the river, at the end of the long, dusty, gravel road that is the main thoroughfare in that portion of the UP, I stopped at a party store and gas station for supplies. This is country dominated by pine forests and cedar swamps, where rusted pickups with gun racks are standard transportation, and the narrow two-tracks leading to hidden cabins, or "camps," are grown over most of the summer with weeds and underbrush, and covered most of the rest of the year with many feet of snow.

The attendant in the store was a young man wearing a stylish haircut and a sleeveless T-shirt. He said he was a native, that he'd spent his entire life near the river. I asked him about its name.

"Hemingway never fished the Two Hearted," he said.

"I know. I'm just curious about the source of the name."

"The French explorers named it, or something," he said. "Well, the Indians named it first, I guess, but the French messed up the translation, or maybe the English messed up the French translation. I forget."

"What was it?" I asked. "What was the original name?"

"I don't know. Something like, 'Place Where the Fat Eels Spawn.' "

Autumn Journeys

IT'S HARD TO STAY INSIDE IN OCTOBER, THAT MOST bittersweet of months. On days when wind and rain are stripping leaves from trees and plastering them like bloody handprints on the ground, I'm grateful to be dry and warm at home. I'm glad for the freshly split and stacked firewood in the garage and the coffee pot in the kitchen and the winter's reading already piled on the shelves beside the fireplace. But I'm soon pacing, watching for signs that the sky will open and the weather break. The year is going down in flames, and I don't want to watch it through a window.

I spend many of autumn's short days tramping through aspen stands, hunting for grouse and woodcock, or fishing for steelhead and salmon in rivers where we can see the fish holding deep in the pools like pods of submarines awaiting orders to advance. And when the weather clears—when the sky turns brittle blue and the wind shifts to the south for the last time, bringing warm, fragrant air from the Gulf of Mexico in a reprieve known mysteriously as Indian summer—I load my canoe on the truck and head for a river.

In October the rivers around here are mostly abandoned,

though the dams and access sites are crowded during the salmon run, and elsewhere you'll see an occasional angler or paddler on a final outing before winter comes. The weather will soon be monumentally uncomfortable, but for a few days you can paddle in shirtsleeves and sneakers. The air has been cleansed by cold and rain, and the low sun cuts through the woods like daggers, pinning your attention to little things. The breeze smells like apples and nuts and faintly of burning leaves. Your perceptions are sharpened. You see and hear better than you did in summer and are too alert to the passing hours to be profligate with them. You might have squandered the summer, when the days stretched out one after another and it was possible to think they would never end. But no-body can squander October.

For me, the month is often distilled to a few unforgettable moments. Such a moment occurred last year when a friend and I floated a section of tag-alder lowlands along the upper Betsie. It was late in the month, the days still warm but the nights so cold they skimmed puddles with ice. The sun was gone that evening, the sky darkening, the river below us shimmering with tarnish stolen from the western horizon.

We had been fishing in a half-serious way, drifting with the current and casting bright streamers to the riffles, hoping a salmon or steelhead or brown trout would strike, content enough when they did not. Just as we entered that uncertain zone between dusk and dark, three things happened simul-taneously: A salmon weighing at least twenty pounds arched silently from the surface of the river below us and hung in the air; a woodcock fluttered from the tag alders, cocked its wings, and shot upriver toward us; and a pack of coyotes began yelping just beyond the hills beside the river.

A moment is a hard thing to capture. It's elusive and stubborn and impossible to predict. Just when you think you've got one nailed down it blends into other moments, and instead of a memory as crisply defined as a jewel's facet, you have nothing but a vague recollection. But that moment on the Betsie was finely etched. It was magical and absolutely unexpected, vivid as a dream, so memorable that it might come back unbidden thirty or forty years from now, when I'm in bed, almost asleep, and have long forgotten that I ever witnessed such a scene.

The salmon reentered the water with a crash that sent spray to the banks, the woodcock passed overhead and disappeared upriver, and the heartbroken sobbing yelps of the coyotes faded. My friend turned to me and said, "Whoa! Too much nature."

He was joking, of course. We can never have too much nature. We barely get enough as it is.

It was nearly dark by then and we still had a few bends to go before we could get off the water. We pushed on, the evening getting colder and darker by the minute. Ahead of us the last traces of daylight smudged the sky and lit the surface of the river with a beckoning glow. We could have gone on all night. We could have followed the river all the way downstream into winter.

Paddling at Dawn

W<small>E CAN GET THERE IN SIX HOURS. THE DISTANCE IS</small> part of the appeal: too far from cities to be crowded, too far from home to be taken lightly. The drive is long but not unpleasantly long, and certainly easier than traveling to true wilderness in Manitoba or Quebec. Gail and I leave home early Friday morning so we can fish most of the afternoon and evening and have camp set and dinner simmering before dark. We have all weekend to explore, loaf, and cast for small-mouth bass. Already we know that we'll wait until the last possible moment to break camp, that we'll paddle to the truck in darkness, that the drive home will take all night Sunday. Monday will be hell, but so what?

Our destination is a cluster of linked backcountry lakes, a diligently guarded remnant of the country the way it used to be. We discovered the place during a period in our lives when we were working too hard and needed frequent escapes on short notice to remind us of what mattered. It's set in national forest, in a region of rolling, rocky hills covered with old-growth and second-growth forests. Some of the pines and hemlocks are 150 feet high and 4 feet across at the base. You can occasionally find giants that have died of old age. Where they have fallen to the ground entire ecosystems live on their decomposing trunks.

The trees are impressive, but the greatest appeal of the place is the lakes—sixty-five of them by informal count, though many are ponds and some are little more than bogs. Ten millennia ago, massive glaciers plowed through here in interesting ways, leaving lakes and ponds behind, sometimes in mazelike congregations. The fifteen largest lakes, from a half mile to a couple of miles in length, are linked by portage trails that form loops requiring a few days or more to traverse by canoe.

At the first lake, Gail and I step out of the truck, road-weary and yawning, and walk down the gravel slope to the water. A breeze brushes the tops of the pines and sets the wavelets sparkling. Walls of evergreens line the shore. We unload our canoe and pack our gear, arranging the Duluth packs and fishing tackle with such care that they become more like components of the canoe than cargo. When we're ready to push off the boat rests level and trim in the water. We step inside and settle onto the wicker seats. With the first stroke of our paddles we are flying.

Not literally, of course. But on this clear water the illusion is striking. The lakes are located at the peak of a divide, with water on the south side draining toward the Mississippi Valley and water on the north draining toward Lake Superior. Because they are fed by deep springs, with no incoming streams, not much nutrient matter finds its way in. The water is said to be chemically identical to rainwater. Anyone who wonders why we need places like this need only look at the water. It's as close to pristine as you'll find.

In a canoe on such water, with the bottom visible thirty feet below, you seem to hover. A single stroke of a paddle and you soar. The slight friction of water against the hull is like the grip of the earth against your bare feet when you were a kid, running so fast across a lawn you were certain you could launch into flight. The pleasure is magnified by the setting—virgin evergreens, rocky shore, scarcity of humans. It's magnified too by the knowledge that you're carrying everything you need to live for a week. If you had to you could last a month. You are independent, self-contained, and mobile. And it doesn't hurt that you're free of computer screens and alarm clocks.

Canoes can be the most practical of craft. On some waters there is no other way to get from place to place. There's something deeply satisfying about paddling the length of a lake, carrying your boat and gear over a trail worn smooth by the feet of the travelers who preceded you, and reaching lakes that are each less visited than the one before. Campsites are smaller, trails less trampled, the quiet more encompassing. We need quiet places, and we need quiet ways to travel in them. We never quite realize how valuable they are until we've been paddling, camping, and fishing in them for a few days. Once cleansed of the residue of daily living, it's possible to find what my son once called "a calm spot" in your heart. It's a good thing to find.

Our weekend will be remembered as a series of fine moments: sitting near the campfire at the end of the day, heat radiating comfort to aching muscles; chopping mushrooms and onions on a slab of silver-gray driftwood; listening to the breeze in the evergreens. We'll remember the way the first loon on the first lake paralleled our progress fifty yards out and mesmerized us with its warbling. Loons are constant companions on uninhabited northern lakes, but they seldom warm to the idea. Like ungracious natives in New England villages, they never miss an opportunity to remind you who is the intruder. This one cut loose with a gargling string of protests, then dived in a fluid twist. It came up two minutes later a quarter mile away, and the rest of the way across the lake we were at truce.

We'll remember the bass that took Gail's popper with a gentle kiss, then pulled with draft-horse power toward bottom. That evening dozens of bass cruised just beneath the surface feeding on beetles and moths, leaving swirls and widening rings up and down the shore. We'll remember the look of the lake in the mornings, when we crawled from the tent and saw the water the way we might have seen it as children—a lake of glass, a mirror the size of a football field, a plain of light and sky fringed by evergreens.

I'm pragmatist enough to think of canoes as tools. I appreciate their grace and elegance, their unpredictability, the way they each seem to develop personality. But I appreciate more their effectiveness in taking me to water other people rarely bother visiting. They're superb tools: They achieve precisely what they're designed to achieve.

But on still summer mornings, with the lake so calm the surface seems poised to shatter, I always discover again the pleasure of paddling for its own sake. I reach forward, slide the blade of my paddle into the water, and pull. It's a virtuous feeling, the reward of muscular activity, of being self-propelled and self-reliant. If the canoe is a good one, light and lithe, it jumps beneath you like a spurred horse.

A good canoe does not merely travel across a lake or river, it glides along the interface between water and air, making hardly a ripple in passing, and is so silent that it blends with the world. Paddling it makes you part of the lake, not an intruder, and a participant in the pastel dramas of dawn. Even if the aesthetics are unimportant—even if you care more about casting deerhair bugs to smallmouths than perfecting your paddling techniques—there is no better way to begin a day.

And maybe that's the key to the appeal of canoeing, camping, fishing, hunting. Being out there is not just a way to greet the new day, it's a way to be reawakened to it, to see it again with the eyes of children.

I often think of a morning long ago, when I was sixteen or seventeen, fishing alone from a canoe on an Ontario lake so muffled with fog that I could see nothing but whiteness in every direction. I hooked an enormous fish, probably a northern pike, that hung deep in the lake, shaking its head the way a large dog shakes its head to fight a leash, then it bulled steadily away, towing me behind. All I could do was kneel in the canoe, hold tightly to the rod, and hope the fish tired. I remember sensations: the power of the fish transmitted like electricity through the rod to my hands, the cool featherlike touch of fog on my cheeks, the motion of the boat being dragged slowly across the lake. I remember feeling part of a drama larger than a single life.

After a while the stout hooks on my lure straightened and the fish escaped. For a long time I sat motionless in the canoe, surrounded by a fog so dense and a silence so complete they seemed to cloak a thousand square miles of forests and lakes. It occurred to me that the water I rested upon had been traveled by canoes for centuries, and that men and women who fashioned hooks from bone and blades from stone had once battled pike like the one I lost. Every person in every age is linked by the things of the earth—the water, the fog, the fish—and a kind of timelessness engulfs us. We are all adrift in a vast, mysterious, unfathomable world, waiting for the fog to lift.

Somewhere on shore, beyond sight, a large animal crashed through the underbrush. Moose! I thought, and my heart launched into flight.

I have never been so full of hope.